Sailing My Shoe to Timbuktu

A Woman's Adventurous Search for Family, Spirit, and Love

JOYCE THOMPSON

HarperSanFrancisco
A Division of HarperCollins*Publishers*

For My Mother

SAILING MY SHOE TO TIMBUKTU: *A Woman's Adventurous Search for Family, Spirit, and Love.* Copyright © 2003 by Joyce Thompson. All rights reserved. Printed in the United States of America. No part of this book may be used or reproduced in any manner whatsoever without written permission except in the case of brief quotations embodied in critical articles and reviews. For information address HarperCollins Publishers, Inc., 10 East 53rd Street, New York, NY 10022.

HarperCollins books may be purchased for educational, business, or sales promotional use. For information please write: Special Markets Department, HarperCollins Publishers, Inc., 10 East 53rd Street, New York, NY 10022.

HarperCollins Web site: http://www.harpercollins.com

HarperCollins®, 📖 ®, and HarperSanFrancisco™ are trademarks of HarperCollins Publishers, Inc.

FIRST EDITION

Library of Congress Cataloging-in-Publication Data is available upon request.
ISBN 0–06–053063–4

03 04 05 06 07 RRD(H) 10 9 8 7 6 5 4 3 2 1

acknowledgments

To those tangible and those invisible beings who helped
me write this book and bring it to market, my deepest
thanks and great affection:

Eggun
Olokun
Schuyler
Ian
Alex
Suzanne
Rebecca
Madrina Maria
Madrina Rosa

foreword

The oldest sentences in this book are nearly two years old today. I wrote them soon after my husband, Schuyler, climbed on an airplane bound for Cuba and an initiation that would give him a new name, Omi Abebe, and a new identity, as a priest of the Afro-Cuban religion called Santeria, or Lucumi. I have been a writer almost as long as I've been able to hold a pencil, but in February of 2001, it had been a long time—seven years—since I had written a book, ten since the last one had been published. This one began as private exploration and not a public act.

My mother, with whom I had walked long shadowy miles through the valley of dementia, was less than a year dead. It was that sad and magical journey, as much as anything, that had brought me to the place I found myself then, on the front porch of the Lucumi religion, wiping my feet on the mat and peering through the partly open door. Once I crossed that threshhold, not only would I no longer be the same person, I would be privy to secrets it was not mine to share. Independence of mind had delivered me to the portal of belief. It struck me as the right time to look back at everything, and everyone, that had brought me to that place. I did this less as an historian, more as a butterfly, respecting strict chronology less than the allure of individual blossoms. Emotional resonance, not continuity in time, gives this little book its structure. I pray you will trust the storyteller enough to share the flight.

More than once, books I have written have served not solely as acts of communication, but as the coin of a special realm where one lives by and for things that are not strictly material. At times when I seemed to have no resources at all, the unexpected sale of subsidiary rights or movie options has paid the rent or bought me time to think and write. My books have given again and again, to me and to my children. This one is no exception. Both psychically and financially, it brought me to my ocha.

On November 2, 2002, in Oakland, California, I was intiated a priest of the orisha Obatala. Today, as I prepare to hand this manuscript to its brave publisher, John Loudon, I am just a little more than two months old.

Iyawo Ala Iku
6 January 2003

1

the repudiation of luck

The journey is unending, but a story needs a start.

Make it New York City, August 1983. Make it that week in August because so many things converged there. I was in New York to meet with a famous movie actor who wanted me to write an original screenplay for him. For several months, we had talked on the phone two or three times a week, each conversation at least an hour long, with no more purpose than to get acquainted. By midsummer, when I was teaching for a week at Clarion, a conference for aspiring science fiction writers, the calls began to include agents and studio executives. Even though I'd never written a screenplay before, the actor wanted to make sure I had a good contract and was well paid for my time.

Luck comes in a flurry, uninvited, undeserved. It defies both probability and logic. The corners of your mouth give off a peculiar, sticky substance, your heart beats fast, and your luck, once it enfolds you, isolates you from your fellows still living by the odds. My Clarion students were titillated by the movie star's persistence, and so, to be honest, was I.

There's more. I had a new novel, my fourth, sold but not yet published, a novel that had come to me in a vision. That's not to say a novel that arrives in this way writes itself. It simply demands to be written. Some parts of the book would go to press exactly as they first flowed from my Bic pen, while others took months of trial and error to find their way. I had laid aside another, more seemingly commercial novel to write this one. Putting oneself in service of a story that wants to be told is a transcendent experience. Voices speak through you, and while you serve them, you are much wiser and more accomplished than you have any right to be, based on your personal history. I labored hard, the book my midwifery delivered felt necessary, and quixotic as the book was, the world welcomed it more warmly than anything else I had ever written.

Earlier that summer, in June, my publisher had held a dinner party in my honor, so I could meet the heads of the various departments who would be preparing and promoting the book. Nine months short of publication, many foreign rights had already been sold. By the time I was in New York in August, two different production companies were vying for the film rights to the novel. Even though he lived in LA and my home at the time was a small town on the northern Oregon coast, one contender had arranged to meet me in New York to pitch his case. I believe to this day he was the victim of an exclusively urban imagination, afraid obscurity might swallow him if he stepped outside the capitals of culture. When my ambitious young editor showed up at my hotel suite to take me out for a celebratory dinner that August, he carried a bottle of good champagne in his briefcase. His toast put in words what the accumulated evidence suggested: "This week, you're the hottest woman writer in the world."

Luck is wry, time's mockery and her test. Somebody had to be the hottest woman writer in the world that week, true, but hearing it was me put terror in my heart.

I was thirty-five years old, the mother of one child and expecting another about the same time my novel would be published. In its defiance of what had otherwise proved to be reliable forms of birth control, this act of conception was as unlikely as my sudden worldly success. I believe now that some souls need to born, just as some books need to be written, and neither has much concern for its impact on the vehicle chosen to bring it into being. The universe was having its way with me that August. And I felt like a fraud.

Because I had written a wise book, people assumed that I was wise. At three months, I looked ripe but not yet pregnant, considerably more shapely than I normally am. The actor said it was my talent that attracted his attention, but with the incisiveness of hindsight, I believe what drew him was something more particular and more complex. I had written a first-person novel in a male voice so convincingly that when he read it, the actor believed I was a man. He had recently starred in a movie in which he acted as a woman. He needed to meet me, I think now, to assure himself that performing a powerful act of cross-gender imagination does not erode one's sexual identity. The first thing he said when we met was, "You're so feminine." Later he wanted to have sex and was offended when I demurred. Have I said already that until that moment I had succeeded in convincing myself our attraction was exclusively cerebral?

Luck is as arbitrary, as chilling as sin.

One August afternoon, in my view-room high above Manhattan, I knelt beside the king-size bed and prayed.

My marriage was neither healthy nor happy. I knew I would be punished for my success. I knew I was shallow and vain. I knew that the wisdom people attributed to me was not my own, nor even accessible to me outside the confines of a story. My good fortune was arbitrary, my self unworthy. I prayed to do no harm.

Like any piece of junk mail, my prayer was addressed to Occupant. I did not know whose help I sought, or how it might come to me. In August of 1983, I had no spiritual center. With that desperate act of scattershot prayer, I set out to look for one.

2

how I was damned

Barbara held the battered Protestant Bible in front of me. Her eyes filled with inquisitorial light. "Swear."

The document whose authenticity she wished me to attest was a scrap of freckled notepaper, on which was penciled JOYCE HAS MY PERMISSION TO SWIM IN PATTYS POOL. SIGNED, MRS. THOMPSON in big fat letters that bore no resemblance to my mother's graceful cursive. Barbara, her little sister my best friend Patty, Ethel who looked after me—we all knew the note was a forgery. Until this moment, trying to pass it off as real had been a game.

With her free hand, Barbara grasped my wrist and placed my dirty little hand on the Bible's cracked black-leather cover. "Swear."

"I don't know that this is such a good idea," Ethel said. "How about we have some milk and cookies?"

Barbara was twelve, a zealot, a born Jesuit. She had more moral authority than any other being in my little universe. Patty and I were her subjects. Her willing slaves. Ethel was a grownup, at least nominally in charge, but next to Barbara's blazing torch, she was a tiny flame.

Beside me, my best friend Patty, ten months younger than I, much braver and a little bit less book-smart, looked worried. I had heard her breathe in when Barbara put my hand on the Bible. So far, she had not exhaled.

"Look, it's clouding over," Ethel said. "It's too cold to go in the pool today."

Barbara's eyes had not left mine, nor had I broken the gaze. I knew we were engaged in an important battle. I do not believe I knew what was at stake. Unexpectedly, she dropped her voice. Soft and sweet now. "Swear."

Surrendering felt like melting. It felt like love. "Okay," I said.

"Okay what?"

"Okay, I swear."

Barbara's hand pinned mine against the book. "Say, I swear on the Bible my mother wrote the note."

"I swear on the Bible my mother wrote the note."

I believe I expected Barbara would reward me. Instead, her brows drew together and her face grew fierce. Ha! That single triumphant syllable seemed to originate from the very core of her. Then her voice gentled into a kind of singsong piety. "Swearing on the Bible to something that's not true is a mortal sin," she said. "Joyce is going to hell for all eternity."

For a moment, we were quiet. Then Ethel said, "She's just a little girl. I don't think God would be that hard on her."

"Six is the age of reason," Barbara said. "At six we become responsible for our sins. Joyce is almost seven," Barbara said.

When I looked sideways and saw the tears that rolled down Patty's cheeks on my behalf, I knew it was true. I was damned.

I don't know if I didn't tell my parents because I was ashamed, or because I was afraid they would try to explain away the exquisite terror and despair I felt. That suffering was my only proof I had a soul, and so, late at night and all alone, I cherished it, folding my hands tightly under my pillow so they would take no sensuous pleasure in the cool smoothness of the pillowcase, my unworthiness a fist-sized ball of ice permanently lodged at the apex of my ribcage, between my stomach and my heart, an enduring presence there.

I believe my trouble sleeping dates from that time.

3

stories remake the world

Eighty acres. Ten bedrooms. Eight children. My grandfather used more dynamite to blast more railroad tunnels through more mountains than any other contractor in the West and never lost a worker. My grandmother picked this sleepy green ridge to live on because it reminded her of Sweden. In his devotion to Mathilde, Olaf filled the big house with the best silver and china and furniture money could buy in the first years of the twentieth century, that ships could bring around the Horn from distant ports. The Olsons were the gentry of Maple Valley, Washington, the huge, whitewashed concrete house with its shaded porches and steep green roof its showplace. Everyone else who stumbles into the stories—the Bohemian neighbors, the Irish, even fellow Scandinavian immigrants—come as rubes and buffoons, envious and admiring of the preeminent clan. Is it any wonder the Olsons kept to themselves?

My mother's family was, first and foremost, a set of stories they told themselves about themselves, stories that gained weight and resonance with every telling. I first heard most of them on those nights my father didn't come home, which meant that he was someplace else, drinking bourbon, arm-wrestling all comers, swapping stories of his own. Out of disappointment and humiliation, my mother the storyteller rose up to weave tales of her magic family, to spin solace and dignity, a bearable reality, on the great wheel of her words. I hated my mother's shame but loved the elegance of her performance, loved being her audience of one. Slowly sipping highballs of her own, drinking continuously without ever getting drunk, anecdote by shapely anecdote my mother evoked a world of heroes and princesses, fine achievements, and noble motives.

At seven, at nine, I never questioned the truth of her stories, or wondered why she needed to tell them, simply let them convince me I came from remarkable stock. Privately, I had some reservations, tiny doubts no more stinging than the brush of a green nettle on a summer's walk in the woods. In the stories, my mother's five brothers—the three uncles I knew and the two who were already dead when I was born—were handsome and clever, whereas the ones I knew in real life seemed rather ordinary. One of them I just plain didn't like. Not one among them was able to step up after the death of his father to save the family fortune from the ruinous Depression. Why not? In the stories, my own father was an irresistible knight errant. My mother loved him absolutely. She loved me. She was not desperately unhappy.

Still, if things didn't quite add up, I figured the error lay with my arithmetic. For years, I believed that the Broadway we lived on in Seattle, Washington, was the same one people called the Great White Way, and wondered why I never saw limousines in the neighborhood, or famous actresses coming out of the movie theatre six blocks from our apartment house. The grownups laughed when I confessed my confusion. For my part, I learned a big lesson: reality is often at odds with our imagination of it. There were at least two streets named Broadway in the world, perhaps many more than that.

The truth, once we see it, seems so obvious.

4

mother's day

Because I lacked the foresight to make reservations, it's three-thirty in the afternoon before my mother and I are seated for our brunch, in the dining room of the biggest department store in a suburban mall. We're in the Totem Room, where the bears and otters and thunderbirds painted on the walls are an uneasy cross in style between Bauhaus and Disney, having very little to do with the native culture they're meant to evoke. At this off-hour, most of our fellow patrons are older women bravely eating alone despite the family holiday, presumably because they did not give birth or their offspring now live in Cincinnati. They have in common unnaturally vibrant hair colors and paperback romance novels, which they read as they pick at their steam-table eggs Benedict. My own children are with their father this weekend.

My mother is eighty years old, still plump, still sharp, still keeping score. She's still able to convey an exquisitely nuanced message— while my arrangements for the day are underwhelming, her innate good sportsmanship prevents her from complaining. It's a stance that doesn't give either one of us much elbowroom for joy. Still, we are trying, doing our best to stave off the boredom and despair that circle our table like wolves who watch in the forest, just beyond reach of the fire's light.

"When are you going to cut your hair?" my mother asks me. "Long hair looks foolish on women in their forties, unless they wear it up."

I can foresee no good outcome from this discussion. With a non sequitur, I try to turn the tide. "Your brother Oscar was your favorite, wasn't he?"

My mother tilts her head quizzically, and the white eyebrows flatten, two slightly separated segments of the same straight line. "Whatever gave you that idea?" she says.

In the wedding album I loved to look at when I was a little girl, my beautiful mother in her white satin gown approaches her groom on the arm of her brother Oscar. She looks like a movie star. He is unsmiling.

"He gave you away. At your wedding. Didn't he?"

"Well, yes," my mother says. "But only because he was the oldest and Dad was dead. You couldn't say we were close." By now, she has a crab Louis in front of her, white meat, pink sauce, great mounds of shredded pale-green lettuce. She lifts a morsel to her mouth, turns it slowly on her tongue before she swallows. "He was awfully serious, you know," she tells me, when she has. "Emmett was the one I had the most fun with."

"What was Oscar like?"

At last she says, "Dour, really."

In the wedding album, my Uncle Oscar resembles a small-town banker. His face is a little puffy, his eyes small, his belly broad. He has what I think of as the Swedish look, something about the jaw that makes men look smug and slightly stupid, a little bit like Goofy, the cartoon dog.

"When I was five, he got drafted in the First World War. When he came back, he shared a house with his army buddy George," my mother said.

My fettuccine Alfredo is filling but tasteless. "Why did he kill himself?" It feels daring to ask, but my mother doesn't rebuff me, only blinks several times behind her glasses.

"The note he left said he couldn't bear for Mom to know." My mother's fork plunges into the greenery, digging for crabmeat. "He'd gotten arrested for drunken driving a second time."

"How could your mother not know her son jumped off a bridge?"

"We never told her," my mother says.

There is a script, and I rarely break from it. If my mother were funnier, I'd be her straight man. In the absence of humor, I'm more like the wall one throws a ball against, faithfully returning each toss until the player grows tired of the game and stops. Today for some reason I am not willing to let my mother stop. "I don't get it," I say.

"We told her Oscar had an accident. Casket was closed. She never knew he drowned."

I know because I have remembered it for more than thirty years that my mother and my father and my Uncle Emmett combed the river, drinking beer and looking for Oscar's body. It was a tidbit from those clinking ice-cube nights of my youth, a time my mother talked about not just what had happened but what it felt like. It was scary and a little bit exciting. The beer made it seem less real, as if they were characters in a hardboiled whodunit. They found him floating like Ophelia, face down in the river reeds.

"Warm that up for you?" The waitress appears with her pot. She pours more coffee. For a moment, we mirror each other, mother and daughter, circling warm mugs with our chilly fingers. The silence grows longer, while I wonder what in the world we will find to talk about next.

And then my mother says, "You know, I've often wondered if Oscar wasn't really my father and not my brother." She says it pretty much the same way she'd say, "I wonder if it's going to rain."

It takes me quite a long time to say anything at all. Is she saying incest, or illegitimate child? On the basis of what evidence does she believe this might be true?

"When did you start wondering?" I ask her.

Over small, shrewd brown eyes, the white brows levitate. "I was in my twenties, I suppose," my mother says. "I think I'll have the cheesecake for dessert."

5

advice from a Christian

It was because of JW that I took a second run at being a Christian. I'd left my children's father by then and set up my single-parent household in the city where my parents lived. The children were one and six. Life was a vast deep ocean and I needed a lifeboat.

JW was the friend of friends. He had been their comrade in arms, first in the civil rights movement, later in opposing the war in Vietnam. He had a thin, knobby New England sort of face, with the high forehead that suggests great intelligence. His sermons were smarter and more challenging than many of his middle-class, middle-brow congregation found quite comfortable. They prided themselves on being politically and theologically liberal, yes, and they did good works in the city, but they were enamored of a spiritual status quo, a baseline disbelief that had no traffic with ecstasy. They held the miraculous, the extraordinary to be not just not real, but not quite socially or intellectually acceptable. To join the United Church of Christ, the denomination from whose pulpit JW preached, it was not even required that one believe that Jesus was the son of God, or had transcended death.

By then a gun-shy Christian, I was glad of the low bar of belief. I was glad that people were friendly and accepting of my single-parent family. Even though I was always a little headachy, with a slightly hollow feeling around my heart by the end of coffee hour early on Sunday afternoons, even though I couldn't help noticing that certain members of the congregation noted for their piety and goodness were sometimes excessively impatient with their children or in small ways mean to their spouses, even though my soul was not particularly touched by the proceedings, I was hungry enough for context that I kept attending and in due time joined.

In addition to this sense of mature compromise, there was the vision of JW walking on the beach, clinging to the hand of his second, younger wife, a breeze off the sea gently lifting up the fine scraggles of his hair, his bony, slightly asymmetrical face suffused by joy. For all his intellectual acumen, for all the breadth of his worldly and ecclesiastical frame of reference, JW had grown up Pentecostal and still harbored the conviction that spirit dwells in flesh, that hormones have their place in faith. That he was willing to let naked rapture shine full voltage from his face proved to me he was a man of considerable courage.

JW recognized me as a seeker. He read some of my books and found worth in them, that mostly unearned wisdom that writing itself put there. About once a month, we met for lunch. I listened and sometimes ventured to give advice when JW talked about his grown children and his relationships with them, damaged when he left their mother for his present, younger wife. That was the price of JW's patience while I asked him hundreds of questions about faith, and grace, and God. I badgered him for reading lists and devoured every text he recommended; I brought him my questions and objections the next time we had lunch, and he treated me with the same seriousness he would have accorded an ardent if immature seminarian, and all of the amusement.

The most important thing JW told me, and he told me this again and again, is that no one ever found faith by reading, or by thinking, or in debate. If God was going to enter my life, he said, it would be at a chakra considerably south of my brain.

6

holding my firstborn

Oregon summer evening, very near solstice. I sit at the kitchen table and look out on the Nehalem estuary fanned out below me, the grassy islands exposed this time of year, the mountain headland gouged with shadow, a thin white froth of ocean just visible above the distant dunes. The long golden light only now begins to stretch toward twilight, first pink barely perceptible, like a faint memory of other sunsets. Tiny, birth-battered, her eyelids waxy, her little belly distended with mother's milk, my firstborn, my daughter, sleeps in my arms. For the first time in my life, I am content.

My husband arrives home from his meeting. His tension shrinks the room a little, changes the density of the air. Beyond the window, languid blue shadows drape themselves across the floating islands.

"You should have put the baby to bed an hour ago," my husband says.

I draw my contentment closer around me, like a shawl, and do nothing. The child is warm in my lap. I watch the unconscious curl of her fingers into a soft fist. Where has she been? Who will she be?

"I said, put the baby to bed." He clatters in the cupboards, in the refrigerator, pouring his nightly wine. That I fail to do his bidding tweaks the ambient tension up another notch or two. Still I resist, an old stone wall in a country garden, hunkered down. He is unused to my resistance.

"You need to observe a schedule," my husband says. "Otherwise she'll get spoiled. She'll run your life."

My baby's hair is fine as the feather fluff on a fledgling goose. Her lips are plump, bowed like a tiny heart. "Such a despot." I say it to her, not him.

I feel the air shift as he comes to stand behind me. I catch the fruity scent of cheap Chablis. "Put her to bed," he says.

Alone, I do what I want to, what I believe is right. Confronted by the willful of this world, I capitulate. I do their bidding. I have always done their bidding. I think it is because they are surer of their right to dominate than I am of my right to resist. Now, although my baby is infinitely mysterious to me, I am entirely certain of what she needs. She needs to sit here with me while I watch the sun's slow setting, mother and daughter breathing deeply, skin to skin, a little sweaty where we touch. I need to hold my baby as the sun goes down.

"Now," he says.

"No."

I say it calmly, in a voice I've never heard before. There is a bit of steel in it, a touch of chill. Although he stands behind me, I can see his anger reflected in the plate-glass window that separates us from the evening outside, a scowl imprinted on the sunset. Then, remarkably, he disappears. I feel the smile that lifts my lips.

Parenthood makes cowards brave.

7

a vocabulary lesson

Etymologically, the word *orisha* reaches these shores from Western Africa, spiritually, from the religion Ifa practiced among the Yoruba people there. None of the English dictionaries I've consulted acknowledges the existence of the word, much less the forces it evokes. Still, I doubt that you are strangers. You, a spiritually alert being. They, God's avatars, owners of the irreducible assets of the planet we jointly inhabit. The ocean, from which arises life. The rivers, sweet waters that sustain us, along whose banks our cities grow. The wind, freeing us from stagnation, blowing in change. Music. Thunder. The forest and the forge. The mountaintop and the marketplace. The cemetery. The division of divinity into knowable aspects is an acknowledgement of how brilliant and unknowable is the mind and energy of Olodumare, God. The orisha, who resemble us, who talk to us, who live among us, give us a way to experience and worship the otherwise inscrutable powers that give us and our environment life.

If God is all of science, then each orisha is one discipline within the whole. If God transcends us, each orisha represents one aspect of who we are and what we can become. We're not talking about monotheism or polytheism here, but about the one made up of many, a spiritual realm reachable by many roads, a community of God.

The complementary word, *ocha,* refers to those orishas who can, through ritual, take up residence in the head of a priest, and to those received by the initiate in the process of "making ocha," or "making saint." Ocha received by santeros are given birth from the ocha of the godparent, in a lineage that extends unbroken for many centuries, through Cuba and so back to Africa. They live in the home of the santero from the time of initiation until his death.

In the New World, orisha worship is known by many names— Lucumi, Regla de Ocha, or Santeria in Cuba, Puerto Rico, and the United States. In Brazil, Candomble. It is possible to learn more about orishas by reading, but the best way to come to know them is to frequent the places they inhabit—the natural world and the houses of their priests.

8

receiving Olokun

For the time it takes two Iyawos, newly initiated priests, to carry the offerings made on my behalf to the sea and return to the house in Oakland, I have the rare gift of Maria's company. We squat on two of a circle of low stools that ring the garage. Several priests who assisted in the ceremonies sit with us, resting and waiting. Maria is my godmother, and theirs. She is a handsome being, with ivory skin and arresting eyes, slightly protuberant and almost black, a color scheme that yields few clues to place or people of origin. As with ethnicity, so with gender. Maria is a riddle. Lean, muscular, with breasts no more than nipples under the wife-beaters she wears with her painter pants on hot summer nights, Maria is a child and a priest of the warrior orisha Oggun. It is Oggun who owns iron, who works the forge and clears the forest, who never rests from work. It is Oggun's tools that make civilization as we know it possible. He is the power that makes the railroad run.

When Oggun rides her in trance possession, Maria's persona, her body language become warriorlike and fiercely male. The rest of the time, she is manifestly woman, executive and artist, butch and motherly, at the same time brash and shy. Maria gives birth to ochas and reads the diloggun. She counsels the troubled and heals the sick. A number of my god sisters are the priestesses of two traditions, santeras and Vodun mambos both, but even in this family of spiritually gifted women, Maria is pre-eminent. She is probably the most powerful woman I have ever known, and one of the most honest. With her partner, Rosa, a priest of Eleggua and an exceptional medium, she heads this spiritual community, this house, this ile.

Today, a Sunday in early December, has been a day of ritual and the hard work that goes with it, ebo meta for Iyawo Aurora Sara, the birthing of Olokun for me. Maria has presided over both. While the cadre of priests who've assisted her look footsore and exhausted, Maria is restless even as she rests. Partly because a draft of fresh air through the open door dissipates it, partly because we've grown accustomed, none of us, I think, still smells the blood of sacrifice.

"Do you have any questions?" she says. "Now's the time to ask."

I have at least a million questions, so many that given this unexpected offer of answers, my questions know of nothing better to do than push and shove each other to be first in line, leaving me tongue-tied, a state in which I too often find myself when dealing with my godmother. I sometimes wonder if Maria thinks I'm stupid. It takes intense good will to bind this family, to be part of it in defiance of every chasm and prejudice that defines the culture that surrounds us. My co-religionists are not my relatives, not my co-workers, not my neighbors, nor am I theirs. Were we not god-kin, we would probably not know each other at all. The orishas are color-blind and indifferent to ethnicity—Maria believes this, and so we try to be.

I've taken long enough concocting a question that Maria simply gives me an unsolicited answer.

"Olokun will help stabilize you," she says. "She'll give you a firm foundation, in your work and your health. She's the keeper of the bottom of the sea. His riches are enormous." Maria grins at the inconsistency of her pronouns. "Olokun is a she," she says, "but she's also a he. She has wives. You know how it is."

The priests giggle a little, reflexively. Whatever is human nature is exaggerated among orisha. Some have two distinct expressions, male and female. Some, like Olokun, slip and slide between the two. After one is used to it, this makes perfect sense.

Three stools away, Mariah, a young priest of the orisha Yemolla, leans forward. "Tell her about the odu, Maria," she says.

In a part of the ceremony I did not attend, Maria cast the cowrie shells in divination. In the resulting odu, my Olokun was born. Maria seems almost reluctant to tell me the results.

"It was Irosun, four," she says. "That's Olokun's natural number. Her most fundamental expression." She looks at me gravely, with a touch of speculation, then leans toward me. "Were any of your relatives lost at sea?"

I can't think of any. "My father stowed away on a fishing boat once. It was during the Depression."

Maria shakes her head slightly. Not what she was looking for. "It was Olokun who gave the Africans safe journey during the Middle Passage," she says. "Who received them when they drowned."

I learned this much in my research. I know that Olokun is an adimu, an orisha which, like the warriors, one can receive without becoming fully initiated. I know she is so powerful and deep that she is not commonly put on the heads of her priests, for fear she would drive them mad, but on their shoulders instead. I nod to show I know a little bit. I nod to show I am willing to learn more. "Someone told me that receiving Olokun really intensified her spiritual life." My sentence rises up at the end, becoming a question.

"Olokun reveals the mysteries we can handle," Maria says. "But she also protects us from the mysteries that are too big for us, the ones that would drive us crazy."

My only response is somatic—a chilly invisible finger stroking my forearm, a sudden tightness in my belly.

Maria sighs. "I read a man once," she says, "and his odu was four four. He'd lived a tragic life. He was washing his car in his driveway and forgot to set the emergency brake. The car rolled backward. It killed his daughter. His marriage fell apart. For a long time, he was lost and bitter. Finally, he got married again, and his new wife had a son. The reading helped him understand what had happened to him. He saw then that the spirit of his daughter came back in his son."

Maria is silent for a moment, and her face is moonlike, a radiant reflection of that man's pain. "Why did that have to happen?" Then she shrugs. "Some things are too hard for us to understand. We'd break ourselves against them. It's Olokun who helps us then."

Into the silence, I spill the story of the novel I'd written, ten years before, how I set out to understand the nature of evil and encountered forces beyond my strength or understanding, how the writing of my novel became entwined with the disappearance and death of my best friend's son. How the experience left me afraid to write again.

Maria takes my story in, turns it over briefly, accepts what I've said without seeming to find it particularly remarkable. I sense without being able to imagine it fully the reality she inhabits—a world of spirit both as complex and as straightforward as the visible, material world. This is not the first time something I, with my skeptic's heritage and Cartesian education, have found fantastic has proved commonplace to Maria. For her, the experiences I've just described fall well within the limits of the ordinary.

"You have protection now," she says simply.

I am left to wonder what against.

9

two Annes

Lastborn of eight, my mother was a whole generation younger than her oldest brother. She went to college, the only of her siblings to do so, during the Great Depression. She drank bootlegged whiskey during Prohibition. She smoked cigarettes when women didn't. She drove her own car. The family dressmaker used patterns from Vogue to dress her at the height of fashion, first as a college girl, then as the lawyer she eventually became. She joined the Prosecutor's Office and was put in charge of divorces and family law. This made her a proponent of the legal rights of women. Because she was photogenic and quotable, the courthouse reporters made her part of their regular beat. If there were no sensational trials to cover, they were happy to let my mother hold forth about deadbeat dads, or how alimony helped divorced women get trained to join the workforce, or occasionally about sex crimes, which she also prosecuted.

My father's mother, who by the time I knew her resembled a barn owl, faithfully kept a scrapbook of press clippings about her daughter-in-law, feature stories accompanied by huge photographs, three columns wide, in which my mother looks for all the world like a movie star impersonating a lawyer. Finer featured, smaller boned, and less boyish, she was the real-life version of the women Katharine Hepburn pretended to be onscreen—modern, capable, a little bit risqué. My father, tall, slender and soulful-looking, was much more attractive than Spencer Tracy. My Parents were law partners before they became life partners. The papers treated their engagement as if it were news, and ran the story with a picture of my mother leaning back in her lawyer's chair, her stylish high-heeled oxfords propped up on the desk, the legs emerging from her fashionably short skirt encased in silky sheen, her fingers tented to suggest she's thinking deeply, while the mischievous glint in her dark eyes suggests that what she contemplates is not the law. My father, seated beside the desk, stares at her calves with a perfect balance of adoration and lust.

This is how my cousins, a generation older than I, remember Anne—smart, glamorous, and spunky, ahead of her time.

The woman I knew best turns up in a photograph taken ten years later, just at the front end of the '50s. The war's over, the men are home, the children of the Depression have already begotten the first baby rumble of the boom to come. The picture is black and white, fine-grained, a square framed in white, with scalloped edges. In the background, against tall windows I barely remember from my childhood home, a little girl sits in profile to the camera, playing intently with something on the table in front of her. So much in the foreground as if she existed in a different plane, a dark-haired woman twists in her chair and leans toward the camera, the corners of her mouth so drawn with sorrow, her eyes so full of longing and lost hope that you wish you could respond to her mute plea and set her free immediately. If I knew who took the picture, I would know to whom my mother prayed for release.

In the picture, she is a mature beauty, face and figure filled out to match the prosperous times, and her hair is shorter, cut and permed to frame her face. Ripeness has replaced the radiance of youth. She still looks like a star, but in a different movie than before. The romantic comedy is over. This picture is a melodrama or a morality play, maybe a ghost story like *Rebecca,* or one of those hard, lush films that Bette Davis made. Whatever the plot, there's no doubt it will leave you crying.

This is the woman I knew for more than forty years. I knew, too, that her sadness had something to do with the girl at the table, against the windows, her only child.

Me.

10

the flight

We sit at the kitchen table, playing War. We've been playing the same game for more than an hour, the piles of cards before us shrinking and growing as our fortunes ebb and flow. My daughter is six years old and wholly engrossed in the game. Numbers and their order are a lesson worth learning. Besides, both the baby and her father are napping and she has me all to herself, something which is all too rare.

It is gray outside the kitchen window, and the river mouth is swollen from an unseasonally rainy autumn, so that the estuary islands have disappeared earlier than usual, drowned till spring. Clouds fluffy and glum as the pelt of a gray fox rub against the far landmass, obscuring the dunes. The gentle predictability of the game is soothing. Inside me certainty grows. This is the day. I can hardly believe it, yet it is even harder to believe that I'll back down. The rest of my life is a huge wave pressing against a fragile dike. I realize I've been waiting for the end of the game, but the game goes on and on, too straightforward and simpleminded for me to lose on purpose. *As soon as the baby wakes up,* I tell myself. *Then.*

"Mommy, play," my daughter commands.

I play. My six takes her two. Her nine wins over my four. At last, I hear the baby whimper, waking. "Put on your shoes and coat," I tell my daughter. "I'm going to change your brother. Then we'll go to the store."

"Can't we finish the game first?" she asks.

"You're too good for me," I say. "I'll never beat you. I give up."

"Don't give up, Mommy."

"We have to get to the store before it closes. I have to buy some things for dinner." I reach across the table and squeeze her little hand. "Shoes. Coat. Now."

"Can I get a treat at the store?" she asks. I tell her we'll see.

I take a moment to pet the dog on our way to the car. By the time I start the engine, my heart's turned from a bee into a wrecking ball, slamming so hard against my chest wall that I can't imagine the neighbors won't come to their windows to see what's wrong, that my husband won't wake up from his nap. Soon enough, we are out of the driveway. Soon enough, we are driving past the store.

"Mommy! Aren't you going to stop?"

I take a deep breath. "You know what? Since it's a holiday, I thought we'd take a little drive. We can go to the store in Seaside for a change."

"I was born in Seaside," my daughter says. "It's a long way away."

"Not so far without traffic. We'll be there before you know it."

The old soul we call the baby has been vested for a bit more than one year in this lifetime. In the rearview mirror I can see him in his carseat behind me, staring contemplatively out the window at the monochrome afternoon. As soon as it's topographically possible to catch a signal, I put the radio on and turn up the volume, hoping sheer noise will keep my daughter from monitoring our course, but even though her reading is still iffy, she knows the terrain. "Mommy! This is where you get off for Seaside," she cries out, as we speed by the exit.

"They have a special on pork chops in Astoria," I tell her. "You know how much you like pork chops."

I am always watching behind me, expecting to see the roving red light of the state patrol. I expect to be arrested, to be taken back. Nothing appears in the mirror except the occasional delivery truck, the errant gas-guzzling passenger car, the camper-trailer on its way home from California. Adrenaline breaks in waves inside me, sickening and exhilarating at the same time. The farther away we get, the less likely it seems that I will turn the car around and go back. I drive deep into old Astoria until I find an ATM. I tell my daughter I need to get money for the pork chops.

Twilight is gray on gray, sucking the last traces of color out of the day. The mist turns to drizzle, still a little too intermittent to keep the wipers on, and a Sunday evening call-in show replaces country western laments on the radio. I surf the dial until I pick up the community college station, playing rock 'n' roll. My daughter turns restless, thrashing inside her seatbelt. *Last chance. Last chance*, I tell myself. My nerves are fixed at a permanent high vibration, above the range of human hearing. I hope my circuit breakers are working. Otherwise I may explode.

"Mommy! Why are we getting on the bridge? Isn't this the way to Grandma and Grandpa's house?"

"You're right," I tell her. "I was going to make it a surprise, but you're much too sharp for me to fool. Won't it be fun to visit Grandma and Grandpa?"

"Why isn't Daddy coming?"

Can I say it out loud? If I say it, it will be true. *Mommy is leaving Daddy. We are running away from home.*

It was a hard summer. It's been a hard fall. It's been a hard eleven years, with just enough sweetness to make me believe my life must not be unbearable.

I have not been entirely alone since early September, when I defied my husband's wishes and drove my stepdaughter, his natural child, to college for the first time. He was ready to let her find her own damn way there—this for the sin of inviting a high school friend to join the family for a last picnic on the beach. He followed us up the driveway, yelling. I drove away. Because my children were there, I came back. Almost as if he sensed my intention, he has not left the house for more than a few minutes, has scarcely left my side for almost three months.

I imagine that people who live at the foot of a volcano fall under a spell like this one. The eruptions are widely spaced enough in time that even though the mountain is always rumbling, even though you are always afraid, you somehow convince yourself it is not essential to move, not quite yet. Just when you least expect it, the volcano blows. Except really, you *always* expect it. Life is flinch. Hope is somebody else's pet.

But this is it. I would rather walk on hot coals than tread the brittle edges of his temper anymore. Who knows how I have chosen this day? Who knows where I've found the courage? Who knows what will become of us?

It's dark now, raining for real. I turn the fan on full so heat will reach the baby in the backseat. My daughter stares at me, still waiting for an answer.

"Mommy's leaving Daddy," I say. It's no secret to this child that our house is not a safe and happy place. I suppose I halfway expect her to be grateful. On the other hand—and I understand this too late—our house is the only home she knows. She starts to cry. Following her lead, sensing her sorrow, the baby, too, starts crying.

And so, at last, do I.

11

my father, his body & the butterflies

I loved my father sober. I hated him drunk. My estimations of his character tend toward the grandiose—hero or shitheel—with no middle ground. Whether he was a good man or not, I suppose I'll never know for sure. When he was dying—his appetite for alcohol having predeceased him by some months—I was of service to him, in much the same way I had been as a child.

Those nights my father was out drinking and my mother was home telling me stories of better days, she maintained her equanimity until he turned up at the door. Then she lost it. Most often, she would break into tears and take refuge in their shared bedroom. My father had usually not eaten since breakfast. Unless he was on the verge of passing out, and it took a tractor-trailer full of booze to bring him to that point in his early middle age, he came home with more appetite for whatever late-night dinner we could cook up between us than for facing my mother and her tears. I remember canned creamed corn, canned roast beef hash and ragout, homemade oyster stew, and T-bone steaks fried briefly in butter, noisy as they sizzled in the old black skillet. He was usually cheerful and tractable—drunk, yes, but not a violent drunk, only occasionally a mean one, that to my mother, not to me. It was my job to bear him company, get him fed and headed toward bed. I hated that part of my daughterly duties far less than those mornings-after that my mother made me go into the bedroom when he was badly hung over and beg him to give up the bottle for good. That was a fool's errand and made us both feel awful.

I was thirty-nine years old when my father began his downward spiral, and had not lived with my parents for more than twenty years, but in extremity, our family reverted to old ways. Faced with a dying man, my mother broke into tears and took refuge in the bedroom. Just as we had skirted the language of addiction for so many years, never saying "drunk" or "bender" out loud, now "death" was excised from our common speech and made taboo. My mother could not bring herself to touch my father's failing flesh, as if mortality was the greatest of his betrayals, and she moved through the house cocooned in a resentful silence as familiar as it was unsettling. In addition to taking him to the doctor's office, or to the hospital for transfusions as long as those helped, apart from shopping and sometimes cooking and tracking down practical nurses, it became my job to groom my father, and to touch him, and to let him say out loud that he was both fed up and afraid.

My father's relationship to his own body was enigmatic. Throughout his teens, he'd been a football player of some civic renown. He boxed in college, losing only one fight ever, and during the Depression he sparred with pros to earn his law school tuition. During the war, at thirty, he played football for the Coast Guard, going head-to-head with men ten years and more his junior. He was proud, almost vain, about his stature and his strength. As athletic prowess waned, his drinking prowess grew. During his waking hours, he smoked constantly, often lighting the next cigarette while the last still burned. It was almost as if he believed sport was a childish thing, meant to be laid aside when manhood conferred its questionable prerogatives. To him, country-club games like golf and tennis were activities for "pantywaists," and he would no more have been caught dead running for pleasure than crocheting afghans. Whether the steady infusions of alcohol and nicotine were meant to approximate endorphins, or if he was simply trying to anesthetize a body aching to perform, is nothing I'll ever know.

In the months that death came courting, a big man shrank, strength ebbed away. With muscle gone, I saw my father resuscitate the gift of will. In those last weeks, traveling by walker from his bed down the hall to his big chair in the living room required immense courage and concentration. For the first time, I caught a shadow-glimpse of the athlete he must once have been. When it grew clear there would be no bodily reprieve, my father accepted his sentence with a combination of resignation and impatience I found quite touching. Often I sat with him as he lay on his side in his bed, too weak to sit up, his lifelong appetite for intercourse with other minds through reading exhausted, every hope, every intention, every diversion sublimed away, so only the waiting was left, and in the end, his native resilience, his stamina, became the enemy, prolonging a condition he found onerous and boring.

In the last days, my father and I each asked the other to make a promise. He asked me to take care of my mother when he was gone. I asked him to find some way to let me know he was all right, after.

My father was a secular humanist long before there was a name for the condition. He professed equal scorn for the carrot of heaven and the stick of hell, believing the harder was the nobler thing—to do right for its own sake. If he ever had firsthand experience of spirits or any reason to suspect that the possibilities of life exceed the coordinates of here and now, he never said so, which doesn't necessarily mean he never did. My favorite aunt paid me three sweet visits after she died, but I kept it to myself, not wanting the rest of the family to think I was insane. I've heard it said of my father's intellectually ambitious parents that they were "socialists with a Ouija board." Whatever his experience of the transcendent may have been, he had no faith to sustain or hope to comfort him in his last days, only a bittersweet dignity derived from renouncing both. Into the atheist's proud resolve, I dropped my request for a message from the other side.

My father lay on his side, and I stretched out beside him, my head propped up on one elbow, so he could look at me without spending too much energy. He had eyebrows bristly as haystacks, the color of flax, and these rose as half-moons above his pale-as-a-March-sky eyes as my words rippled out between us. In the seconds of silence before he answered me, I sensed that he was processing a lifetime's data. Then, a faint sweet smile. "Well, okay. Sure," my father said. It was not quite three days later that he died.

It was summer then, and I sat outside with my coffee in the backyard where he'd liked to sit and smoke with his. Since he'd been ill, the squirrels he fed with peanuts had stopped coming round. Birds sang, I'm sure, bees buzzed as they went about the work of pollination, bloom to bloom, even the sunlight probably vibrated to some energetic frequency of its own, but the yard seemed very still. Then in its middle, out of seeming nowhere, appeared the largest butterfly I've ever seen, a swallowtail navigating the slight summer breeze, a butterfly stately and substantial as a frigate embroidering the air with its dips and swirls. Before it began to perform, the butterfly purposefully invaded my visual range a time or two, sallying near until I couldn't help but notice, close enough that I could feel the displacement of air by wings against my skin, and then retreated to the center of the yard, which was, implicitly, its stage.

My attention focused on the swallowtail as minutely as if an unseen cinematographer had just pulled focus and altered my depth of field to exclude everything that might distract me from its dance. How long did I watch—the smooth, sweeping arcs, the curlicues, the hops and darts—before I thought to call my mother? I was afraid that if I moved my body or withdrew my gaze, the butterfly would disappear, but when I returned with my mother after the hiatus of at least a minute, he was still there. For a moment, he hovered above her head, and then began to dance again, as artfully as before. It was beautiful, and filled me with benign excitement. At the end of the movement, after it took an airborne bow, the butterfly perched for a moment on my shoulder, then flew up and over the laurel hedge, away.

When it was clear that the show was over, no encores, I told my mother about my father's promise.

"I know what you're thinking," she said, "but I can't believe that's true."

"But you saw it yourself," I said.

"I saw a butterfly in the backyard," she said. "That's all."

For the next three days, my life filled up with butterflies. I raised my eyes and saw two dozen of them, poised with wings spread wide on the frizzy purple blossoms of a Japanese lilac as I walked up the street. If I talked to a friend in the open air, soon butterflies flew between us and landed on my shoulders or my hands. When my gaze went long in contemplation, butterflies called my attention back with their antics. They encircled my children like prayers. It was not the season for swallowtail migration. No one else I knew was similarly afflicted. At last, a poet friend told me that in the days immediately after her grandmother's death, her mother was incessantly surrounded by white moths. Not an uncommon vehicle for souls in transit, according to my friend. So many cultures believed.

I told my mother this.

"Believe what you need to," my mother said. "I can't."

"Can't or won't?" I asked her.

"Doesn't matter," she said.

Seven years later, on the anniversary of my father's death, I was making coffee in my mother's kitchen when I had the fleeting impression of motion outside the window—surprising because she lived in an environment free of wildlife and peeping toms alike, on the thirteenth floor of a downtown highrise. When I went to investigate, I found a swallowtail butterfly dancing in the airshaft beyond the glass. I called my mother to come and see.

She glanced briefly at the butterfly. "Oh, that," she said. "It's been there since this morning."

"Come on, Mom," I said. "Doesn't it make a believer out of you?"

My mother closed and locked the window, then shut the curtains for good measure. Suddenly, it was dim in the kitchen, the light low and brown. My mother turned her back toward the window. "No," she said.

12

a speculation about the silence of God

If I were your mother, I would have told you long ago that there's a secret door between your body and your soul, most easily opened, for most of us, in the act of making love. And then, since it's my mother-credo to do no harm, I'd add—"or in erotic communion with a fellow human whom you hold in high regard." I wouldn't want you hobbled by romanticism, or held to such impossibly high ideals that you never went looking for your door.

If I were your mother, I would also warn you to beware of buildings that claim to be the houses of God. I heard it said once, jokily, that on their days off, when they are not actively intervening in human affairs or shoring up the sweetness of the earth, the orishas get together in a little apartment in a poor section of Havana around a very big screen television and laugh themselves silly at the unceasing soap opera that is our lives, all the while puffing on good Cuban cigars and swigging cheap rum. And, darling, whether you imagine one big white distant god or many more particular brown ones who like their little pleasures, I would tell you to get off your butt and out of the house if you want to make contact. If you go to a mausoleum, you'll find dead bodies. Livings gods inhabit a living world.

The big spiritual question of our time is so ridiculously simple that anybody with a black suit and a theology degree is embarrassed even to say it out loud: How come God doesn't talk to people anymore?

Religious professionals, with their real estate deeds and company-owned cars, have a lot of fancy and non-intuitive reasons for God's silence, most of which come down to the idea that we're not worth talking to. Our forebears found *their* secret doors, naughty them, and we, naughty us, sneaked through; we greedily ate the best apple; we were arrogant or ungrateful or negligent in our devotions. We forgot to pay the phone bill and got disconnected.

The fact is, we've been calling the wrong number for a long time. The right number is always the same, and it's not in the book. It passes on through word of mouth, whispered by one generation in the ear of the next. If the right number is forgotten, or willfully suppressed, we're out of luck, and out of touch, and hopelessly out of sorts, as well.

The number, I think, is a spiritual technology, one that works because the interface is exquisitely designed, with one plug perfectly adapted to the human—that whole klugey and inspired tangle of neurons, of organs, tissues, and blood and bone—and one that fits the divine. Since I've held this hypothesis, which arose as an attempt to make sense of empirical evidence, I've witnessed one spiritual technology that unfailingly makes the connection between parties, and others which, sharing some elements of the successful paradigm, are partially successful.

Based on the evidence of religious texts, based on the universality of certain icons, based on the eerie similarity of the stories people have always told about themselves and their relationships to the world and to their gods, there's good reason to suspect that many tribes and traditions in many parts of the planet once had their own open line. One 800 number, many local exchanges. Virtually every human society has stories of those good old days when gods and humans freely exchanged gifts, favors, and information. Virtually every society has a matching story of how that privileged intercourse was lost. Virtually every society mythically equates the loss of Eden with the birth of guilt.

• • •

Julian Jaynes, one of the few academics willing to work from the premise that the once-upon-a-time of human/divine communication might just be true, suggests that the loss of connection between humans and gods happened as the world grew larger and more complex. His notion, somewhat deformed, I think, by the shadow of the ghost of Freud, suggests that "god" in primitive local societies was something like a deified superego, and that humans really did (or really thought they did) perceive its voice addressing them directly on a regular basis, an experience he guessed might be something like the auditory hallucinations experienced by modern-day schizophrenics. When tribes who hallucinated one god or set of gods eventually came into contact with other humans who hallucinated other, different gods, Jaynes suggests, the stress on poor humans' ambiguity tolerance was so profound that it jump-started nothing less than a shift of consciousness, from collective to individual, us to me. God-talk was a casualty of this brutal transit.

I hope I've not done too much violence to Jaynes's ideas. I honor them both for their willingness to take the loss of communion with God seriously and the ingenuity of his proposed explanation for it. Still, on the basis of nothing more authoritative than personal experience, I believe he got a few things wrong.

What Julian Jaynes got right—that gods are local. But I believe they're local in the sense that they inhabit a geographical, ecological place, rather than in their attachment to a particular kinship group. Gods arise from and dwell in particular features and forces of the geophysical landscape—in the winds, in the woods, in the mountains, in waters salt and tidal or sweet and flowing. They inhere in their world-niches independent of whether there happens to be human society nearby to interact with them. These local gods are, if you will, the forces that shaped the planet and continue to be its metabolism, and nothing in them is irreconcilably at odds with those same forces described in scientific rather than anecdotal language.

I believe that humans, at least those of a spiritual bent, are innately sensitive to the presence of these local gods, these gods in nature. No matter what our heads know about the nature of God, the hairs on the back of our necks tell us when we are in the presence of the divine. With our whole selves, we recognize holy places when we step into them.

Human residents of holy places establish give-and-take relationships with resident gods. I believe any human group that doesn't categorically deny its own spiritual nature and its basic spiritual gifts will in time come to learn the language of the gods, as those gods will come to understand the needs of the people who share their habitat. Just as there are natural athletes among us, born organizers, talented artists, builders, and political leaders, so every tribe has its spiritually adept members, its shamans, whose special ability it is to tend to the communal relationship with the divine. Not every person needs to possess every power and predilection expressed in the group as a whole. Not every person has to know God for the tribe to understand collectively that God exists and is essentially friendly.

Perhaps, and here I step beyond what I personally intuit to be true into the realm of what *might* be true, the spiritually gifted members of our tribes, our spiritual ancestors, accrue sufficient magical capital in their lifetimes that with death they pass from human status into a kind of divinity of their own; they become our tribal representatives to the pantheon of place and, in due time, as the world grows large and complicated, to the godhead of the whole planet. Thus spirit begets spirit, god begets god, and with this intermingling, this constant commerce between our contiguous worlds, we are able not just to talk back and forth but to collaborate in a mutually sustaining state of symbiosis. This is a kind of chicken-and-egg scrambled version of Mark Twain's observation that God created man in his own image and man, being a gentleman, returned the compliment. Frivolity aside, it makes profound evolutionary sense that humans and their gods should be reciprocal creations, that their sustained interaction should promote survival, that from that interaction should arise new permutations of spiritual aptitude.

It might have happened just this way.

As to Julian Jaynes's assertion that psychological pressures resulting from the perception of a larger, more diverse world, a world possessed of many gods, was responsible for the muteness if not the death of God, consider the counterexample of the ancient and highly sophisticated religions of the West Africans, first as they traded among themselves, then ultimately as they traveled on the slave ships of the middle passage to various new homes in the New World. Whether the point of origin was Yorubaland or Dahomey, whether the destination was Haiti or Cuba or Brazil, these religious systems, and the ritual technologies associated with them, not only traveled brilliantly but proved hardy and inventive in challenging new landscapes. Not only were their adherents able to perform the necessary acts of syncretization to appease the slaveholders and their priests, they were able to domesticate the native gods of new places. One among the orishas of the Yoruba, Ochosi the hunter, has among his designated tasks the translation of spiritual messages between gods in passage and gods of place. This is an act of diplomacy, not capitulation, stunning for its matter-of-fact recognition not only that different places give birth to different gods, but that all gods of the planet are at some essential level kin.

It appears to be one of history's whopping good jokes that the most oppressed peoples were able to preserve their relationship to God intact in the face of diaspora, cultural multiplicity, and the degradations of slavery, while ascendant groups sacrificed their authentic spirituality in the act of making religion a tool for achieving and maintaining political and economic dominance. Spiritual technologies driven underground, out of the sight and hearing of the dominant culture, became treasures to revere, preserve, and protect.

While they underwent cosmetic adaptations in order to survive, the basic beliefs and rituals were never subject to changes aimed at cowing the faithful and shoring up the power of the religious elite. The Judeo-Christian story of battles in heaven between God and his ambitious angels might be a parable of the history of the church in its many guises doing battle with God himself for control of the hearts and minds of humankind. At least here on earth, it would seem to be the hubris of angels, far more than the sins of ordinary men and women, that cost us our intimacy with the divine.

Those who exploited God for personal aggrandizement lost touch with God. Those who depended on their gods for physical and cultural survival, who kept them safe from co-optation, could still get through. The lost-but-wanting-not-to-be, the God-hungry, have to look in radically unexpected places if they would connect to the divine. The historical keepers of those places must, despite skepticism, mistrust, or disinclination, open the secret doors to all who come in peace.

13

my husband becomes a priest

My husband is in Havana, becoming a priest of Yemolla, orisha of the ocean. Yemolla is nurturing and stern and all-encompassing. She is deep and mysterious, the mother of us all.

Lacking clairvoyance, I can only imagine the house in Havana where my husband sits, helpless as a baby, in his process of rebirth. I imagine the room is dim, the light brown, the air hot and a little sticky, and I imagine my husband is exhausted, now his heart is wholly open, now that his long-awaited initiation has finally come to pass. I know that his head has been shaved, that he is wearing white clothes. I do not know if they will let him write while he is on the throne.

I know my imaginings are only that.

In the three weeks he has been gone, I have listened but I have not been able to hear his voice. Only once has he turned up in a dream. Much of the time, I've felt his absence as palpably as his presence has been part of my life in the five and a half years since we met. He is part of me, but he is gone now. See? There's his winter coat, his running shoes, his wallet. The copper pan I cook my oatmeal in is his. Faint, familiar, the scent of him lingers in the pillowcases and the towels.

Once I woke in the middle of the night to find the room filled with the citrus and cinnamon scent of Florida Water, an old fashioned cologne often used in ritual baths.

Thoughts come to me—Remember to lock the door, light the candles; the ancestors would like a cup of coffee; be kind to yourself today—but I don't know whether they're my thoughts or not.

What comes to me in his absence is great rolling waves of emotion. I have been writing hard, in these weeks, about painful things. I have done my best to be present in my body, doing yoga, running, eating only foods that honor health. I have drawn breath like spring cleaning into the shady recesses of my soul. Last Saturday night, I could not stop crying. I sat in candlelight at my ancestors' altar, weeping inconsolably, rocking gently, almost hypnotically side to side for the visceral comfort that such motion brings, not frightened by the intensity of the sadness that poured through me, but impressed by its power and how profoundly old it seemed. And I was pleased with myself for pursuing my regimen so faithfully and fearlessly that it produced this letting go.

When I was fifteen, my parents encouraged me to join them in the habit of smoking so I would stop complaining about their smoking. Only half-jokingly, I say that upon my achieving adolescence, my family handed me a carton of smokes and a lighter and said, *Here, dear—this is how we deal with strong emotions.* For the next thirty years, I followed instructions, sucking every slight and sorrow, every fear and doubt and disappointment, every ruptured ideal and bruised dream up deep inside my body. I managed my central nervous system, my metabolism, and most of all my emotions with the great god nicotine. When I stopped smoking almost four years ago, I found that my emotional development had been chemically arrested just at the point I took up the habit. I was fifteen years old again, self-righteous, innocent, and insecure, with only an adolescent's immature defenses against some very grown-up challenges.

The point being, last Saturday night, I had every reason to believe my very cells were filled to brimming with thirty-plus years of grief and elation, that my spiritual/physical practice was paying off in their torrential release. What I was experiencing seemed a lot like how friends who've had breakdowns described their breakdowns, except that I felt protected and was not afraid. Perhaps, I speculated, I would be able to have the healing effects that follow emotional cataclysm without lingering too long in the valley of the shadow of the broken-down. My heart is not breaking, I assured myself; it's breaking open. This seemed right. After hours of weeping, between one moment and the next, my tears stopped and a numb exhaustion overcame me, sleep hard on its heels. It was for all the world like passing out, except there was no alcohol, no drugs involved.

The next morning I felt light as a feather. Wanting to work with my body, not my mind, I began to clean up the clutter my husband had left behind as he headed off for his transformation. Instead of resenting it a little, as I had the week before, I embraced rigorous housecleaning as a gift both to him and to myself. I packed away the colored clothing he would not wear for the iyawo year he'd spend in white. I vacuumed and dusted and readied the floor where he'd be sleeping when he returned. I bought the first daffodils and put some in every room. The heavy seas I'd sailed the night before were calm now, and I was happy at my simple chores.

Early that afternoon, the phone rang. It was one of my godsisters, fresh out of Cuba with news of my husband. At the fundamental drumming the night before, Yemolla had mounted her priestess and told my husband he needed to visit the ocean. Her biggest message for him, on the eve of his initiation, was that he must let go. *Let go.* When they took him to the ocean, it was very emotional, she said. My godsister is a priestess of Oya, orisha of the wind. She was sure that the breaking open I'd experienced the night before was related to my husband's opening and not entirely my own.

I was of two hearts—one sad to think I was not the author of my own experience, the other awed at the possibility of such deep connection on the wires of true love. When the house was as clean as I could make it, I ran to the beach and cleansed myself with sea-water, paid my respects to my soon-to-be mother-in-law. I knew this was what I was supposed to do, but the knowing was my own. I was relieved it should be so.

The next morning, Monday, my husband's ritual initiation was to begin. It was a bright morning on Bainbridge Island, tinged with the last of winter's chill, and I went to the park to have a run. I was well into the second mile, my legs feeling both strong in motion and as warm and cosseted as if they still rested between the soft sheets of my bed. Breathing was easy and my mind was as free of thoughts as it ever gets. I remember expecting to run for a long time. Suddenly, in the backstretch where the trail is level and runs past a grove of third-growth firs, a wind reared up and blew my hair back, pasted my running clothes against my body, insisted, finally, that I sit down on a narrow scallop of grass between trees and trail and be quiet. The impulse was as irresistible as the rush to cover when an earthquake starts. I am a respecter of the lessons of the wind. I sat.

I sat cross-legged, hands on my knees, open palms up, in the most reverential posture I know. Hazy sunlight, scarcely yellow at all, shone through a little window of white haze in the gray sky. The wind fell away. A bird sang in the stillness. My attention was compelled. Things stirred at the place inside my ribcage I think of as my heart's address, things too deep and primitive to wear the names we give emotions. They moved. I wept. Then I was released, knowing I had been present for a holy moment in Havana. I ran on, wondering how my husband and I had become as closely linked as twins, how we would learn to embrace our dual citizenship in the magical and ordinary worlds.

14

getting rid of the gun

Words did my mother's bidding, but things defeated her. She could not throw them away. Much of her house in Seattle's Seward Park neighborhood was furnished from her family's home at Maple Valley. The workshop where no one worked and the space under the staircase were filled with boxes that hadn't been opened for twenty-five years. After my father died, my mother gave in to her own peculiar combination of mourning and inertia, simply, mostly silently, coexisting with her things. Every week, I offered to help her excavate the premises. For months on end, she refused me. Finally, one late-fall day she nodded yes, and the work began.

In the most unlikely places, we found empty bourbon bottles my dad had drained and neglected to throw away, and full ones he'd cached against times of drought and forgotten all about. Hidden among rusty, old-fashioned tools in the workshop, we found my father's service revolver, a sleek, mean-looking metal sculpture reposing on blue satin in a wooden case. My mother had always taken a non-negotiable position: no handguns in the house. When we found the revolver, she was beside herself.

"He swore he got rid of it," she said.

"We'll get rid of it now," I said.

"How?" she said.

"Sell it."

"We can't sell it. It's unlicensed."

"We'll say we found it."

"I can't let people know the gun-control judge kept an unlicensed handgun."

"Let's throw it away, then."

"Teenagers would find it in the dump. They'd rob a convenience store."

"I'll hide it inside something else," I said, remembering finding this same gun or another in the back of my mother's closet when I was little, tucked inside one of a pair of riding boots she never wore, remembering how illicit, how dangerous it felt to come upon it there.

My mom was still heavy enough then that her jowls jiggled a bit when she shook her head. "Absolutely not. What are we going to do?"

I volunteered to call the police station and ask how to dispose of an unwanted firearm.

"No names," my mother said. "Promise me you'll never give your name or his."

I made up a story. My uncle had just died. I was his heir. Cleaning out his things, I'd happened on the gun. Because I had two children, I didn't want to keep it in my house. Please, Mister Officer, what should I do?

Just bring it on in to the station, Little Lady. Glad to oblige.

When I did, the enthusiasm of the sergeant on duty for the revolver was almost sexual. He lifted it reverently from the case, sighted along its barrel, ran his hands over it, opened the chamber, clicked it shut, all the while making little sounds of hardware appreciation deep in his throat. "A mighty fine piece," he told me. "How about you sell it to me instead of turning it in?"

"Well, I—"

"How much you want for it?"

I was torn between saying I'd pay him to take it off my hands and wanting to see what he'd offer.

"How about, say, two hundred?" he said.

The desk cop, hairy and middle-aged, with a Hanuman monkey face, spoke up. "He's trying to take advantage of you, Miss. That's a nice gun. Don't sell it cheap."

"Oh, all right," the sergeant said, pulling out a wad of money so big in diameter I couldn't imagine where in his pants he could concealed it. The bills he peeled off were fifties. "Five hundred."

"He'll pay more," the desk man said, but I'd already chirped, "Sold." I handed over the revolver in its fancy box and left the station grinning, with ten bills still warm from the cop's body in the pocket of my jeans.

When I handed over the wad of cash and told the tale, I expected my mother to be amused, but she wasn't, really. The next labor of her widowhood had already commenced—how to sneak a probate file back into the County Clerk's office without alerting anyone to its long absence. My father was, evidently, a couple of decades derelict in his responsibilities as the court-appointed trustee of the estate. To my mother, so long used to sweeping up behind him, neither mailing the file back nor tossing it in the trash was an option. She was already seeking a third, more complicated way.

"How come Dad was so determined to hang on to that gun, anyway?" I asked her.

Her answer was a long time coming. "His friend Andy called him henpecked when your father told him I wanted him to get rid of it. Only I'm sure he used a different expression."

"Like what?" I asked.

"Pussy-whipped," my mother said.

"Machismo," I said.

"There are some things about your father you don't know," my mother said. She pushed the stack of fifty-dollar bills across the table at me. "You can keep the money," she said. "I don't want it."

I was a single mother with two kids to feed. I folded the five hundred back up again and put it in my jeans.

15

the use and misuse of stories

Once when my daughter was ten, I taught at a weeklong arts camp for ten-year-olds. Half of the teachers were writers like me. Half were storytellers. We worked in mixed teams, the writers helping kids make up the stories, the tellers showing them how to turn them into performance pieces, with words unchanging, every gesture, every expression, each inflection scripted, practiced, and perfected. I'd never given much thought to oral storytelling before that, but once I did, I saw that it was my mother's art form. She kept a whole arsenal of anecdotes that were perfectly made, just like the tales the tellers told, so well-polished that she knew just when to pause to let her listeners laugh, where the peaks and valleys of the telling were, how to build suspense, how to hold an audience hostage for a long time with a string of several stories stitched together.

Some of her best stories I came to hate, because they cast my mother as heroine, me as buffoon. They were of the most-embarrassing-moment genre, mostly—my mother being the one who was embarrassed, I being the cause of her embarrassment. There was the Violin Recital, where that painfully chubby music student gets up on stage and forgets her piece. There was the Painfully Earnest Adolescent with her passionate, misguided convictions. When I'd long been a size-four adult, my mother still took pleasure in telling the one about how excruciating it was to take me shopping for Dancing Class Dresses, because I was so hefty, and how I once modeled Chubette Fashions on a local television show. There was the Skating Lesson, where I fell down so many times my mother had to stop counting, and the one where she woke up from childbirth only to find I had a Floppy Ear.

Imagine my consternation: that was the theme.

When I was little, I assumed my mother dominated every conversation because of her superior wit and charm. Later, I saw she was something of a bully, aggressively holding possession of the floor against all comers. Her stories were her soldiers and her weapons. At that point, without saying so out loud, I was embarrassed for her. Later still, as I corrected the learned disability in myself, I saw her manic anecdotalism as the crutch of someone who had never learned to listen. Me, I almost wept with relief when I learned that conversation was a collaborative form, but it was a concept my mother never really grasped.

In their decades together, my parents had reached a sort of accommodation—my mother holding forth, my father hiding out—in a way that kept their world in near-perfect equilibrium. None of the wealthy widows in my mother's new widowhood home at the Grosvenor House was willing to replace him as her captive audience. She had a thousand reasons why she didn't want to mingle with those women—they were shallow, or Republican, materialist, nosy, ignorant or interested in opera—but it slowly grew clear to me that these were no more than a preemptive strike against rejection.

Through the dense weave of her excuses, it was just possible to glimpse the social hurts I never actually saw inflicted. People spurned my mother in the Grosvenor House dining room, closing ranks around a vacant seat, because they preferred conversational exchange to soliloquy, no matter how amusingly delivered. After she rebuffed the first few openhearted invitations, failed to return the friendly phone calls, they ceased to come her way. My mother had no idea how to be.

For eight long years, she studied loneliness, while I learned the limitations of filial devotion. It was not for lack of trying that I failed to make my mother happy. It was not for lack of trying that she failed to push me and my children away.

16

surrogates

Adeline

My mother's oldest sister, my Aunt Adeline, came first, so early I don't remember her contributions. It was she who took care of me the first weeks after birth, who gave me bottles and baths and taught my skin to trust. By example, the whole of her long life taught that to be of service, cheerfully, is to be fulfilled. She also taught me it does no harm to boil the bejesus out of your gravy.

When she was ready to surrender her nursing duties and move back home, to her own house and garden, to my Uncle Sig, she hired Ethel and passed me on to her.

Ethel

It starts with the outfit, a quilted blue skirt made from a whole circle of fabric and a white sweater piped at neck and cuffs with blue and red. I twirl in front of the mirror, delighted with my image in my new clothes. Then I hug Ethel and kiss her cheek, menopause-damp and scented with face powder, the kind that comes loose in a box with fans on it. "It's beautiful. Thank you."

"It *does* look cute on you," Ethel says. It's the first time she's ever bought me clothes, and she's clearly pleased to have pleased me. "Why don't you put on some white socks and your black shoes?" she says.

"How come?"

Ethel's pink face lights up. "It's bingo night."

My heart drops. If Ethel goes to bingo, I'll be left alone with Chet, her husband. This is not my idea of a good time. I'm nearly ten, and I already know a lot of things, like Chet is not nearly as smart as Ethel, or as refined, that she treats him more like a child than she does me. Their apartment, Number Twenty-two in the building that my parents own, is close tonight with the yeasty memory of this afternoon's baking, the hot oil Ethel fried dinner's shoestrings in, the constant low note of Chesterfield straights smoked end to end. My parents have gone away to the state capital for three whole months and Ethel is in charge of me. I wouldn't have it any other way.

With Ethel in charge, my life is gloriously predictable one day to the next. I have only one dinner, with Chet at five-thirty, no second, late-night meal when my prodigal father turns up hungry. I'm in bed by nine-fifteen every night. Ethel and I stay together in my parents' apartment, Number Three, and leave Chet to snore away upstairs. I have a real breakfast every morning. On weekends, I can have a friend from school stay overnight. Ethel loves to brush my long red hair, and I love it when she does.

For as far back as I have memories, Ethel is part of them. According to the stories of my elders, I was just a few weeks old when she came. Originally she was hired to take care of the housework and the apartment building so Mrs. Thompson could look after the baby. That, the grownups say, laughing, lasted about a day and a half. Nobody has ever officially added a word like *nanny* to her job title, and as far as I know, Ethel has never complained about the added responsibilities. Because Chet was gassed in France during the First World War, he wasn't able to give her the baby she always wanted. Things work out. Even when my parents are at home, I spend a lot more time with Ethel than I do with them.

"Socks and shoes," Ethel says. "I don't want to miss the bus."

Slowly the clues begin to fit. "You mean . . . ?"

Ethel blows out a long white snake of smoke. "That's right. You're coming with me."

First I jump up and down a few times. Then I ask her if my mother said it was okay.

"I thought it could be our little secret," Ethel says.

My parents never ride the bus. I am allowed to take it downtown by myself in the daytime, but never at night. I don't believe I've ever ridden on a bus that was lighted up inside before. There are fewer older women with shopping bags at this hour, and more tired-looking men. Ethel lets me sit by the window and I watch the dusky streets for a while before she touches my shoulder and I turn to look at her.

"Do me a little favor?" she says.

"What is it?" I ask.

"Well, I told a little lie," she says. "I told some of the girls at the bingo game you were my daughter."

The world lurches a little on its axis, not too much. My mother is beautiful and educated and aloof. I love Ethel, love her as much as I love to breathe or eat cinnamon rolls, but she is not my mother.

"So I was wondering if you could maybe just pretend it was true. Just for tonight." I can still hear exactly the way she said those words, casual and pleading at the same time.

I take the question as stated: quite seriously. My own identity may be rather complicated, my emotions ambivalent, but at least I know my part. I was born to it, after all. Am I capable of convincingly pretending to be somebody I am not?

"You mean, like, you want me to call you 'Mom'?"

"Well, yes. Could you?"

Two big waves of feeling rise up then. One is a feeling of disloyalty to my real mother. The other, I'm ashamed to admit, is snobbery. My mother is a lawyer. She has better things to do with her time than look after kids. Still, the chance to play a part has its appeal. And Ethel seems to want it very much. "Well?" Ethel says.

"How about if you say, 'This is my *girl*'? People will think it means daughter, only it won't be lying. I *am* your girl."

Ethel gives me a squeeze.

"I'll hold your hand," I tell her. "I don't know if I can say 'Mom' or not."

The bingo game is in the parish hall of St. Joseph's Catholic Church. It's crowded and noisy, and one of the first things I think is that I've never seen so many people who look like Ethel, by which I suppose I mean, not like my mother. People who are not young, not beautiful, not stylish or well off. They do seem content to be themselves, and to be here, though, and a good number of them seem glad to see Ethel as we pay the cashier and then pick out our cards and go to the refreshment bar to get coffee for Ethel and Kool-Aid for me.

Hands full, Ethel leads us to a long folding table occupied by her special friends. One woman, Gloria, has saved two folding chairs for us. Everyone at the table stares at me so hard I feel my cheeks get red. Before we sit down, Ethel says, "Everybody, this is my girl, Joyce." She says their names, too, and I nod politely, once at each one. The master of ceremonies coughs into his microphone and we sit down, spreading out our cards, eight for Ethel, two for me. In whispers, she explains how to play the game. As soon as the caller calls out the first number, people bend over their cards, and the hall grows silent. I get the hang of it fast, and pretty soon Ethel passes me over two of her cards to watch so I won't get bored.

At intermission, Ethel picks up her coffee cup and gets on line for a refill. I tag along and stand at her elbow. Then a woman comes up to us, the sort of woman who leads with her chest, aggressively. Her eyebrows are drawn on with a black crayon, and there's something funny about the way her mouth stretches sideways when she talks. It looks like she gets her hair done, like my mother does. Ethel does her own hair, thin Swedish blonde, and mine. The woman is wearing a plaid skirt and a brown sweater over a white blouse. She peers at me as though I were a kind of dog she'd never seen before.

"I'm Mrs. Nordby," she says. "And who might you be?"

"This is my girl," Ethel says. "This is Joyce."

Mrs. Nordby peers harder, and I get the feeling she doesn't like Ethel very much. "I didn't know you had a girl," she says.

"Hello, Mrs. Nordby," I say.

Mrs. Nordby nods. Studies us and says to Ethel, "Is she adopted, then? She doesn't look much like you."

Ethel's face is shiny, pushing past pink on into magenta. I look up at Mrs. Nordby. "I take after my father," I tell her, which is no lie.

"Well, Ethel," the old bag says, "you're certainly full of surprises."

If I had to throw up right now, I'd make sure I got it on that woman's shoes. As it is, I tug at Ethel's hand, pulling her away from the encounter. "Come on, Mom. I changed my mind. I want to get a cookie before the Blackout starts."

"Excuse us, Hester," Ethel says. "My girl is hungry."

Ethel bought me two cookies and went on to split the Eagle pot three ways. That night was pretty much a microcosm of our whole relationship, a love that stayed a little bit illicit until Ethel was dying and I held her hand and stroked her hair and told her she really was my mother after all, while my real mother paced impatiently outside the ICU, occasionally sticking her head in to ask if I was ready to leave yet. An hour after I did, Ethel died.

She didn't teach me where to look for God. She did teach me to accept love wherever it's offered, to give love wherever it's needed. If I've been a good mother to my own children, it is her legacy.

Aunt Kate

My great-aunt Kate lived alone in a big old house she called Tree-tops, perched on the edge of a deep ravine. Inside, Treetops was full of filtered sunlight and cool brown hush. The furniture was dark, the décor exotic, full of charming oddities Kate had brought home from a round-the-world junket with her spinster sister, Maude—a lacquered teapot shaped like a lotus blossom, a cage for crickets, three tiny carved ivory elephants, the brass statue of a stork perched on the back of a tortoise, a wonderful box carved of aromatic black wood that had no obvious means of opening, a wooden tray inlaid with mother-of-pearl. I remember Persian carpets, a tall soft four-poster in Kate's upstairs bedroom, a gleaming banister descending floor to floor with no curves, an unusually deep, trough-like kitchen sink, and on virtually every surface in every room, Kate's houseplants.

Other people I knew grew African violets on their window sills, or avocado plants in terra-cotta pots, but Aunt Kate created tiny vegetable worlds. Each of her dish-gardens was planted with several kinds of flora, various in height and width and in the colors and shapes of leaves. Among them she created hills, bridges, streams, and valleys. In this landscape, Buddha meditated beside a still pond. Here Chinese sages walked a winding path, apparently deep in conversation. Tiny carved birds hid amidst the foliage and it was my delight to find them there. I tiptoed from garden to garden, stalking the little statues as softly as if I really believed they'd startle and fly away if I were noisy or abrupt. This was good practice for the stillness I needed later, when Kate let me feed the squirrels that visited her kitchen window, offering them nuts and grains from my open palm.

Kate collected and ate wild greens and mushrooms. She belonged to the Audubon Society and kept a life list of birds she'd seen and heard sing. Fur in coats and feathers on hats, she found immoral. Sometimes when I spent the night with her, she let me come on her long early-morning rambles through the ravine as she collected wildflowers and paid social calls on the trees she truly loved. In spring, she gave me nasturtium seeds to plant; in winter, a wire feeder to fill with suet for the birds that didn't fly south. During the school year, she took me to nature films at the Paramount Theatre downtown. In the warm darkness, I often fell asleep in my plush seat and dreamed of flying. Every gift-giving occasion brought another book on how to make the stars, or the shellfish, or the trees my friends. Twenty years later, Kate might have been a gentle vegan, a respected member of a community of like-minded hippie peers. In the early '50s, though, most folks, family among them, found her a little cracked.

I knew Aunt Kate was magical. She lived alone, but was not lonely. Too many fellow creatures visited regularly and depended upon her generosity. She talked to them and they talked to her, sometimes in English, sometimes in thrush, or crow, or squirrel. She could tell you the botanical name of every tree and shrub in her ravine, but that was only information. At a deeper level, she knew them for the living beings they were, creatures with personal histories, individual quirks, unique strengths and challenges to overcome. When I was very little, I saved a bag of leaves fallen from my favorite birch, thinking the tree might need them to stay warm, thinking I needed them to remember summer. Kate laughed, but not at me. She was wise in the seasons, and taught me that the cycles of life should be celebrated and not feared.

Physically, she was fine-boned and small. Her gray-shot hair fell past her waist when she set it free at night. During the day, it nested like a great egg in the billow that framed her face. Kate had the high family forehead, coupled with her own small beaky nose and pointed chin. After forty years in the classroom, she wore the sturdiest, most sensible shoes and dresses in the same drab spectrum of grays and browns that nature chooses for female ducks and geese. Pictures of the young normal school graduate show a delicate beauty with the hint of a smile in her eyes, as if the photographer had been a special friend. The Aunt Kate I knew looked and moved like a sparrow. After she had a stroke and lost the power of speech, she sat in her wheelchair at the home we put her in and cooed, cawed, and chortled all day long. The nurses called her the Bird Lady.

Aunt Kate taught me to look to nature to find God. She taught me how. She was the first person I loved who died.

Grandma Thompson

Between her husband's passing and the time she broke her hip and lost her mind, my dad's mother lived down the hall from us, in Apartment One, the first of several relatives to take up residence there in the transitional time between independence and death. From Grandma Thompson, I learned wry humor and long-suffering, how to be humble and independent-minded at the same time, how to make the best of a bad deal, and how to tie my shoes.

It was my job to check in with her every day to make sure she was still alive. It was her job to pretend she didn't know that's why I visited her every day. Even though Grandma Thompson was a retired teacher and I wanted to learn to read more than anything in the whole world, my mother for some reason believed it was better to start first grade with an untutored mind, so Grandma read out loud to me or told me stories about the time she spent in Alaska, in the middle of the Bering Sea, from 1908 to 1910. I still have the letters she wrote home in those years. Someday in her honor I will go there and see Little Diomede Island for myself.

Olga

A late-spring evening in the parking lot of an upscale family restaurant in a Connecticut bedroom suburb of New York. Whenever members of our Northwest family cross the continental divide, they end up here in Westport, checking out my cousin Carol Ann's big white house with the gold-plated flatware and the dining room that seats twenty. Her husband, Jack, can be counted on for a restaurant meal or two, and Carol Ann, who cooks like a butter-loving angel, always makes at least one memorable feast during a family visit. My college roommate and I have stayed in their guest room a couple of times this spring, while we pounded the pavement and worked the phones, trying to scare up our first jobs in New York City. It's 1970, and the economy is limping along, disproving the adage that war begets prosperity. Tonight, my Uncle Lee and his new wife are in Westport, too. The meal we just finished went on Jack's expense account.

My Aunt Olga is one scant year dead. My Aunt Adeline is, by all reports, heartbroken by Lee's hasty remarriage but determined to be courteous. My cousins, Olga's daughters, are not done mourning their mother, but truth told, they may be a little bit relieved to have their widowed father provided with built-in companionship, laundry service, and kitchen help that isn't them. My mother is just plain pissed off. She has not yet spoken to the new wife, nor will she ever. After a longish dinner in the company of the bride, I'm pretty much forced to conclude my mother isn't missing much.

Jack makes sure my scotch on the rocks never gets warm or runs dry, but even the buzz this brings on doesn't dull the heart bruise of Olga's absence. Olga was my godmother. She had a springtime spirit, as fresh and soft as the new growth on a fir tree, as quick to giggle as a stream full of snowmelt, as full of unexpected rainbows as an April afternoon. Even now, when I see lambs or calves or colts wobbling

joyously on their new legs in roadside fields, it calls her up. She
could make anything grow. She could make anything fun. She met
the world with her senses open, and by example instructed me in the
joys of smell and taste and color. We walked in the woods and on the
beach together. We made up stories and poems. We fed her chickens,
collected eggs, and candled them. I helped warm her nest as her two
daughters flew away into their own lives, and she was my favorite
playmate, at least until I was six years old and allowed to play with
Patty, the girl next door.

My Uncle Lee's new wife is one of those almost-elderly women
who look upholstered. Her hair is dyed and teased and lacquered,
and she wears her big bejeweled glasses on a leash around her neck.
She is not what you would call a free thinker. Her opinions, charted,
would fall precisely in the middle of the middle of the bell-curve
bulge. I gather she used to work in a bank. Is this where they met?
My Uncle Lee appears delighted to have found himself a mate who
makes him seem incisive. Now and then, he reaches for her hand. I
can't help noticing the red nail polish and the big diamond ring. My
Aunt Olga's wedding ring was modest to begin with and wore thin
with work and time.

Because my mother has given herself permission to be flat-out
rude to this woman, I am not. I sit, I listen, I pass the rolls, all the
while aware that she's aware I'm the snubber's daughter. With no
memories and no loyalties, my roommate is much more gracious
than I manage to be, and I let myself take vicarious credit for her
good manners.

Even though my roommate and I can both hold our own in a
college drink-off, that's merely beer. Carol Ann and Jack have eighteen years on us and out-scotch us two to one. As faces flush and con-
sonants begin to soften, they turn the conversation to the courtship
of the newlyweds. Uncle Lee and his wife tell the tale in tandem, call
and response, with her evoking and him agreeing. My god, I don't

believe it. Either I'm very drunk, or they just admitted they started dating while Olga was in the hospital, dying from cancer.

I must look horrified, because the bride says, "Lee was so lonely. He was just like a little boy. If I hadn't come along, he probably would have starved."

Au contraire, I mutter inside my head. *Some other bloodsucking gold-digger would have turned up instead.* Having sold his dairy farm for tract housing, my Uncle Lee might, in certain mercenary circles, be considered one hell of a catch.

Somebody, I hope not me, says the thing about a man's heart and his stomach, and we all make those little too-full-by-half noises that pass for laughter this time of night. Then Carol Ann sighs.

"I wish that were true," she says. "With all the food I've put in this man's stomach, he should worship the ground I walk on."

Jack laughs uneasily. So do we all. But she's not done.

"Twenty years of marriage, eight children," she says, "and do you realize Jack's never once said he loves me?"

It's a conversation stopper, that. Leads us to pass on after-dinner drinks. Makes us want to get the check and get out of there.

"Every birthday. Every anniversary," Carol Ann says. "Every Valentine's Day. Just once in my life I want to hear it come out of his mouth."

Jack's mouth is pursed as if he's sucking on a Preparation H suppository. Now I'm pissed off. She was a genuine high school prom-queen beauty. He got her pregnant. "Just tell her, damn it," I mutter. "What can it hurt you?" Only I'm not sure anybody actually hears me, since we're all scraping our chairs back, getting up, rustling.

So here we are, back in the parking lot, trudging across the asphalt in layered couples—Lee and his bride in the lead, my room-mate and I a little woozy in the middle distance, our host and hostess bringing up the sullen rear. Twilight's melting down to darkness. It's warm and still. Nobody seems to have any words left worth saying. A premonition of tomorrow morning's headache knocks at my temple. And then it happens.

There is no breeze and no storm brewing, but suddenly something like an electrical current passes over my cheeks and my arms, making the little hairs stand up and the nerve endings sing. It is a touch like silver, spookier than sex. A voice speaks clearly inside my head. It says, "Go catch up with your uncle and give him a hug. Tell him you wish him happiness. *I* do." The voice belongs to my Aunt Olga.

I catch up with my uncle. I give him a hug. I wish him happiness.

I feel a little after-tingle, and then she's gone.

My Aunt Olga taught me a lot of things, but this was, perhaps, the most singular. She visited me twice more, differently, before she disappeared for good.

17

a prayer for love

One late-fall weekend, a friend and I were teaching a writing workshop at the beach. The theme of the workshop was transformation, and we were both determined that each and every one of our students should be transformed by the experience. By late Sunday afternoon when we sent them home, we'd done our job. Each participant was at least a little different than the person who'd turned up on Friday night. We, on the other hand, were exhausted and cranky, unchanged except for our sense of net depletion.

Even though, perhaps because, a cold dense rain was falling, we decided to go to the beach. Frustration drove us to walk fast. Words spilled out with equal force. My friend was in a relationship with a woman when she fell in love with a man. It seemed perfectly reasonable to her that as long as there was no duplicity involved, she should be able to enjoy both relationships in long-term equilibrium. Neither of her lovers agreed. As we leaned into the hard wet wind, my friend told me how sick she was of people confusing sex with politics and reducing human options to either/or. Not only did her girlfriend feel betrayed, her editor, who had defined my friend as a Lesbian Writer, was furious that her heart would not conform to her place in the catalog. My friend wanted nothing less than the absolute freedom to be herself.

Another mile of trudging the heavy wet sands and we got to the real heart of her matter. For years, my friend had been trying to write a novel that grew out of real family stories. It didn't take the disapproval of her relatives to derail the project because a powerful censor was already resident in her own heart. It froze her up, shut her down, left her unable to write. At those rare times when she was able to break through the layers of constraint, she was able only to write badly. Once again, what she so ardently desired was the freedom of her own identity. She wanted to claim the stories that were by birthright hers to tell. Wanted to tell them. Her wish was simple and it was formidable. And it was out at last, syllables of steam spoken into the cold, wet November afternoon.

Suddenly, my friend stopped walking and turned to me. "What do *you* want?" she said.

Now I set our pace, and it was furious as I tried to outwalk a thousand superstitions. I was just shy of forty then, and for all but a few years of my life, I'd been responsible to and for other people; it was axiomatic that their needs came first. The notion of wanting something for myself and saying so was less liberating than frightening, an act of hubris sure to attract the negative attention of the gods. Of what gods, I was not sure. That wanting would be punished felt like gospel truth. Besides, what was to want? My children were bright, healthy, and loving. Sometime in my second year of divorced single-motherhood, I realized that I was no longer in psychic pain, which was not exactly the same thing as contentment, but a definite improvement on crying all the time. Money was tight, but I had a book of good short stories coming out.

"Well?" my friend said.

"Love," I said.

"What? I can't hear you over the surf."

"Love," I said.

"Did you say love?"

"Sort of," I said.

"What do you mean, sort of?" my friend said.

"It's never brought me anything but trouble," I said. "I'm not sure I'm ready to be hurt again."

"You want a different kind of love," my friend said.

"Yes," I said. "I suppose I do."

My friend's hair was plastered to her head and her face was shiny with the rain. The day was graying fast toward dusk, and against that monochrome backdrop her dark eyes were almost crazily intense. "Let's tell the ocean what we want," she said.

"I used to throw rocks in the ocean and make wishes," I said. "If the rock I'm throwing reaches the water's edge before the next wave breaks, I will live happily ever after."

"No you won't," my friend said. "But let's do it anyway."

She stood at the edge of the tide, wave-froth lapping the toes of her boots, arms spread out wide. "I want the time and the money and the courage to write my novel." She yelled it due west, toward the blank horizon. If her wish kept flying, the first land mass it reached would be Japan. She added a few qualifiers after that: She wanted the novel to be brilliant and get good reviews. She wanted to make enough money from it to buy a new car. A new-to-her car, she amended. From that, I concluded she, too, feared over-reaching. When she turned back toward me, a bright red spot sat atop each cheekbone. I couldn't tell if the tears streaming from the outer corners of her eyes were caused by wind or sorrow.

"Your turn," she said.

I told myself I was still trying to formulate the proper syntax. Surely it matters how you say what you want. And I didn't want to leave anything out and regret it later, or ask for more than I could handle. Was it legitimate to ask for love without any of the displacements and discomforts I had good reason to associate with it?

"Go on," my friend said.

I sidled up to the tideline.

"Face the water," my friend said.

I tried, but every time I managed to swivel my body front and center, my nerve failed and I turned sideways again. Maybe I seemed smaller that way. Maybe I thought I was invisible. Maybe the ocean wouldn't take me seriously. I truly was afraid of fucking up.

"You know, I'm not sure I'm ready for this after all," I said. "Besides, it's almost dark. How about some hot chocolate?"

"Chicken."

"Well, yes. Faced with it, I'm not sure what to ask for."

"Ask for your soulmate," my friend suggested.

That seemed general enough to keep me out of error's way. Gingerly, I turned toward the water and muttered, "I want my soulmate." Turned back to my friend. "There," I said.

"Without prejudice as to race, age, gender, or ethnic origin," my friend instructed me.

"That's a mouthful."

"You don't want to close the door on something good just because you can't imagine it right this minute, do you?"

I supposed I didn't. I turned back to the ocean, the roiling, thunderous, spray-teasing, almost-black-as-night-was-falling ocean with her white-crowned peaks and gullies stiff as dark meringue. That ocean. My gaze lengthened toward infinity and my ears rang. Everywhere my skin was exposed, the wind blasted it with needling spray. I repeated the politically correct equal-opportunity soulmate clause. The wind blew my words back into my mouth so promptly and forcefully I wondered if they counted as said.

18

the Indian spirit & the failed novel

Facing west, NeahKahNie Mountain is a sheer slab of black basalt, rising straight up from the Pacific Ocean. North, south, and east, erosion has turned rock to fertile soil and dressed the mountain in cool, shadowy forest and grass meadows June-dense with wildflowers and scrubby stiff salal. At its summit, the mountain has a knife-edge spine and on each side falls as sharply from it as a blanket strung upon a taut rope.

One cannot walk this trail without understanding the consequences of a misstep. To see what happens to a rock kicked loose by your boot is to feel alive in every organ, and grateful to be that way. It makes you stop, and breathe, and listen. The air is always cool and sweet, with a salt tang, and into the silent top space above the ocean's distant deep bass rumble a bird is sure to sing then, each note so clear and round and *present* it's hard to believe you can't see as well as hear it. When you can't feel your heart slamming anymore, it's time to choose—to go on, carefully, prayerfully, to the end of the trail, or to sit down right here, which is a sensible enough choice, like standing pat in blackjack when you're holding seventeen. Here is beautiful, and if the day is clear, you can see a hundred miles due south.

To go on is to climb and dip steeply on a trail just slightly wider than your boot until you're standing in the sky itself, the only thing to the west of you that imaginary line where blue meets blue, where planet and atmosphere converge. The trail widens a little here at the end, enough for two people to sit, or one to lie flat against this jumping-off place, this last heady scrap of the continent before everything dissolves into the journey out.

When I lived on the Oregon coast, this was my aerie, my safe and sacred place. Whatever was happening in the yellow house that looked out on the estuary, it was only an hour's hard climb from there to here. More often than not, reaching here, I became irresistibly sleepy, stretched out on the loose dirt and rocks of the promontory, and surrendered consciousness for awhile, feeling entirely safe in doing so. I woke up stronger, relaxed and refreshed and something else, too, sexually energized by sun and wind on my skin, by sheer height, by the faint buzzing sound, not just of flies or sunshine but of every atom of the earth and air. I wanted to make love to the whole earth then, and in a kind of microcosm, I sometimes did, hitting the top on the top, then falling away, melting into the surrounding blue.

Objectively speaking, NeahKahNie Mountain is the highest coastal headland on the Pacific from the Golden Gate to Alaska. It was the last and most difficult stretch of the Pacific Coast Highway to be completed. The Nehalem tribe, which dispersed in winter, gathered in summer in the great meadow scooped out of the mountain's southern flank for games and celebrations. In their name for the mountain sounds their name for the divine.

KahNie was a young god when his parents were called away to a great gathering of all the tribal gods of the region at Mount Rainier. They left him in charge of the mountain and of the Nehalem tribe. KahNie, like capricious Jehovah of Old Testament stories, got angry because the people didn't pay him enough honor or, one suspects, cough up sufficient offerings to satisfy his adolescent pride. He built a huge fire on the side of the mountain, heated the rocks until they were red-hot, then scooped them up and tossed them into the sea below.

What had been glassily calm water till then was set to churning and roiling by the hot rocks. The Nehalems' canoes, which had glided on the sea like swans or skaters on a pond, were suddenly at risk in the surf, and the fish which heretofore had leapt out of the water and onto the beach now had to be trapped in nets or speared. Where life had been easy and the riches of the earth abundant, now everything was hard and scarce and dangerous. The mountain lies at the heart of the tribe's loss-of-Eden tale.

The coming of European settlers was hard on the Nehalems. Disease took a big toll. So did alcohol and economic exile. The very last member of the tribe, an elderly woman, died soon after I moved to the area in the late seventies. And KahNie was left alone on the mountain, a god without a people, which is why, I think, he was always so accessible to me—to anyone who happened by.

Near Easter, hundreds of acres of tulips burst into bloom on the flower farms of the Skagit River Valley in western Washington state. One spring not long into her widowhood, when my mother was cranky but not yet demented, she and my children and I climbed in my car and headed north to see them. On the way, we had a little contretemps. My mom told one of her stories that turned upon my insufficiencies. I asked her nicely to please retire it from her repertory. She went into a deep punitive sulk that lasted for miles and miles. Finally, I asked if she was still mad at me. It wasn't a question she could answer yes or no; she took it as an invitation to have ourselves a wingding. And what is that? An imprecise word for a performance piece of guilt and shame, disappointment, accusation, apology, protestations of innocence and love. One of the key plotpoints of any wingding in which my mother was involved had to do with the failure of the other party to intuit her true desires and her emotional state and act accordingly. Thus it was not a genre that could ever have a win/win outcome; the only role available to those who joined in the improvisation was villain.

That day, it went something like this.

ME (attempting jollity): So, are you still mad at me?

MY MOM (sniffs back snot): What do you expect? You. . . .

ME (exiting traffic to park on the shoulder): I'll tell you what. . . .

MY MOM (alarmed): What are you doing? Is something wrong with the car?

ME (cheerful): Nothing's wrong with the car. How about we sit here until you stop being mad?

MY MOM (processing—alarm, comprehension, resignation): Oh, for heaven's sake, drive.

If I'd always had the self-possession to behave with such level calm, we might have had an easier time of it. My response salvaged that day nicely. Spared the emotional ravages of a blowout, my mother actually relaxed and enjoyed herself. We drove around the countryside, admiring the tulips; checked into a motel; ate heartily; went to a movie. That night, my kids shared a bed and I slept with my mom. Near dawn, I fell into a dream.

I am holding a small book in my hands. The paper is thin and fine. I struggle to read the text. Even as I do, the letters of the words turn into flowers, pink and white, one by one, until the pages are in bloom, and once the last line on the righthand page has flowered, the lines of flowers spiral up like a tornado, spinning themselves into a pillar of flowers that reaches up to heaven.

It was a breathtaking sequence, and as I woke from it into the morning light, two words spoke themselves inside my mind: Paradise Illustrated. I took it for a title. I took the whole dream for an assignment.

My publisher had no interest in a comic novel about West Coast New Age spirituality. I had no interest in writing the mystery/thriller the company wanted from me. The previous book, which I'd intended to be (and still think is) a "real" novel exploring the nature of evil, did fairly well for them and nearly killed me. My editor cheerfully but firmly informed me that I could go ahead and write *Paradise Illustrated* if I felt I had to, but I still owed him a scary book when it was done.

Even now I couldn't tell you to what personality flaw or foible my intransigence in the matter should rightly be attributed. Nonetheless, I went AWOL on an existing book contract in order to fulfill the assignment I'd received in my Easter dream. I believed this was what I was supposed to do. At that time, I wholeheartedly believed that people who do what they're supposed to are rewarded for it. I also believed that since the book had been "assigned" to me, it was ready to come into the world, with me as its vehicle.

Second-guessing karma, as it turns out, is always a bad idea.

KahNie tried hard to find his way into *Paradise Illustrated*.

The narrator, Judith, meets him when hiking on his mountain one day. They converse, then cavort. Judith agrees to take him home with her. KahNie's journey through the greedy New Age '90s let me turn an innocent's eye on a jaded society. His adolescent arrogance and his sexual prowess were always causing problems. And he was a god, with an array of godlike powers. Because the divine energy of the physical world was as much as I had empirically experienced of God, I didn't see this as pure metaphor. If I believed in anything, I believed in KahNie and his kin. My story simply gave him legs.

When the KahNie version of the book was done, a fellow writer agreed to take a look. Her credentials—ethicist, church deacon, ex-wife of a genuine New Age guru—made her seem like the ideal critic, and she was generous enough to have at my bulky manuscript.

One of her criticisms—that humor based on making fun of other people is cruel—hit its mark and humbled me, even though I'm glad enough she was never asked to edit Twain or Shakespeare. Her other, equally emphatic objection was that one simply cannot and must not mix up magic and the real world. Write fantasy or write realism, she said, but don't try to make them coexist. Her implicit message was, There is no magic afoot in the world.

What about magical realism? I asked.

To my esteemed critic, that plea was available only to writers of Latin American descent. It was simply incompatible with middle-class North American experience. For any number of reasons, I let myself be convinced that she was right. Removing KahNie from the novel felt like murdering a friend and caused a certain sadness to hang like ground fog over subsequent drafts. Magical realism gave way to good old real-world social activism. The leaps of faith required to believe in that were much more intellectually defensible. My novel died of its own extreme ambivalence, not before I'd spent two solid years of my life and all my savings trying to make it work. With it expired my appetite for storytelling and my willingness to live by fiction for one day more.

It was time to go to work for Microsoft. And so I did.

19

the last blind date

Of the five consecutive assignments that filled my three and a half years as a Microsoft permatemp, four were good jobs. The fifth was toxic. This job I chose myself, over safer, duller alternatives, because it so perfectly replicated in the sphere of work the psychological dynamic of my romantic relationships. My boss was creative, charming, and full of himself. On every project, he had himself one "golden girl," a smart, talented woman who acted as his muse, confidante, and general workhorse. When the going got rough, as it always seemed to with this man, the workhorse became the scapegoat and was sacrificed for the good of the team. As for me, the hook was yet another chance to be the exception. He wasn't going to fire *me*.

On the day I first heard my husband's voice, I had just been dismissed from that job via answering machine. Two days earlier, my thirteen-year-old Honda station wagon had ended its life as a working machine. That morning, I'd gotten a call from my mother's doctor, saying her mammogram showed irregularities and he suspected a recurrence of cancer. Could I bring her in for a biopsy right away? My children continued to expect my services as nurturer, problem solver, banker, chauffeur, and cook. On the brighter side, a colleague from a previous project had just tipped me off to an opening on a new one. I had a chance at it if I got my paperwork to the program manager by the end of the day. When the phone rang at ten to five, I'd just finished updating my résumé. If I hadn't been expecting my son to check in, I wouldn't have answered at all.

The voice was male. It belonged to the friend of a friend, someone I'd never met. For months, I'd been dealing with people in brusque, role-related, task-specific snippets. This man sounded as if his entire personality were present and available right then. Perhaps because I had some vague recollection of being that sort of person, I found it unsettling. Besides, he was one slow talker.

"What time do you have?" I asked him.

"Four fifty-seven, but I might be fast." Pause, then, "Ashley told me you have a job at Microsoft," he said.

"Not anymore. Not unless I get my résumé emailed over there by five."

"She suggested we should get together and talk sometime," the slow talker slowly said. It must have taken him a whole minute to get it out. With 120 seconds of the official workday left, it was suddenly more than I could handle.

"Call me back sometime, okay?" I said. "I'm hanging up now."

A week later, I had a new job and an approved loan at a too-high interest rate for a new used car. My mother had had her biopsy. While the new lump was malignant, it was also completely encapsulated and might stay that way for years without spreading. She had a choice between a mastectomy and vigilance. Given that she was a poor risk for surgery, she chose to wait and see. At the doctor's office, she remembered little of her previous bout with breast cancer—neither the year nor the type of treatment she'd received then—but I took that as a natural side effect of her Don't Ask, Don't Tell relationship with her own body.

Once all the fires in my life were put out, I had the leisure to regret my rudeness to the friend of my friend. Needless to say, he'd not called back. In a spirit of *Why the hell not?* I decided to call him. It wasn't as if men were lining up outside my front door. It had been almost a year since the demise of my last small affair, with a bass player too many years my junior.

Mr. Slow Talker's number was in the book. Fortunately, it was his machine that answered. I left a message saying I was not normally a raving bitch. If he wanted to have coffee sometime, I was game.

I wore white shorts, a white tank top, a white linen vest. It was dressy attire for Microsoft in August. My new used car didn't have air-conditioning, and by the time I found the address on Queen Anne Hill that evening, everything about me was damp. A last-minute check in the rearview mirror showed a pink and shiny face. Not sure if I'd own up to my nicotine habit or not, I pumped breath spray all the way down to my tonsillectomy scars, then climbed up from the street to the little house at the top of an ill-kept rockery, the shrubs rangy and dry. The front door was on the side of the house, beyond a little strip of cement porch. It stood open. Inside at first glance was dim and looked serene. There was no immediate sign of habitation, beyond three rather nasty-looking carved masks that leered at me from the side of one bookcase and a glass of wine that stood by itself, half full, on a table by the windows. Music was playing, but I don't remember what it was. When I knocked on the door frame and stuck my head inside to call hello, I found that the air was wearing dinner for perfume.

The voice from the telephone traveled around a corner or two to tell me to come in and make myself comfortable. The temperature drop was startling as I stepped inside. Coolness settled like a silk sheet on my damp skin, drying my sweat so quickly it made the fine hairs rise along my arms. The shock to my pupils was equally intense. I was still in the thrall of purely sensory impressions when my host appeared from the back of the house. I remember hoping on my way there I would not find him unsightly. The sound of his voice had conjured someone portly, but this man was rather tall and rather slim. He was wearing clean blue jeans and a white shirt with the sleeves rolled up. His sockless ankles looked pale and touchingly thin as they descended into black loafers. A longish shock of medium-brown hair. The glint of spectacles. Finally I dared to look at his face. Open. Pleasant. Intelligent.

All of this was perfectly ordinary blind-date processing. Then my vision ratcheted a little, as if the scene were being projected and the film had just skipped a frame or two. Inside my mind, a voice said, *So this is what he looks like this time around.* A velvety silence engulfed the moment. Then everything was back to normal. Even the plate of little golden cakes on the floor inside the front door seemed quite normal. A whole platter piled with the same confection rested on a low and richly decorated table that appeared to be some kind of altar. *What a quaint place to keep dessert,* I thought.

My host extended his hand. "I'm Schuyler," he said. "Can I get you anything to drink?"

I handed over the two bottles of Pinot Grigiot I'd picked up at Fred Meyer. We went into the kitchen and watched the fish stew bubble gently in its pot.

"I wrote a novel about a guy named Schuyler once," I said. "It was a long time ago."

"I know," Schuyler said.

"You do?"

"Uh-huh. I liked the book, but the author's photo was kind of scary. I like the one on *Bones* better."

"You read that, too?"

"Research. I'm a journalist."

"Amazing."

He shrugged. "You know, the day your Schuyler learns he's inherited the merry-go-round is my birthday. March 16."

"Is that the day? I don't remember."

"I'm glad you look like the picture on *Bones*," he said. Then he picked up a sizeable stack of pages and handed them over. "These are for you."

"What are they?"

"Tit for tat," he said. "I read you. Now you have to read me." He grinned. "Don't worry. They're good."

I agreed to take them home with me. I told him about all the strange and magical coincidences that had already occurred in the context of the novel *Merry-Go-Round* and the real merry-go-round on which I'd based the one in the book. Finally, I said, "You know, the Schuyler I wrote is pretty much who I'd be if I were a man."

"I figured that," he said. "Would you like to see my garden?"

The plot he farmed was in the nearby public garden. We took a bottle of wine and a pack of cigarettes to the P-Patch with us. A brisk hot wind blew up around us. It animated leaves and flowers, billowed in our clothes, and lifted up our hair. Twilight was long and touched with purple. Schuyler's garden was well laid out, well tended, full of esoteric edible plants like golden raspberries, artichokes, Tuscan cabbage, and chard. Raked by that rich light, caressed by that warm wind, my workday shell washed away by cool dry wine, I felt as if we existed in a painting, realistic and romantic, not quite modern. We seemed a little more vibrant, a little more dangerous than life.

There was no dessert but talk that night. Schuyler had baked the golden cakes, but not for us. They were an offering to Ochun, the orisha whose provinces are eros and art.

The next day on the bus I read his stories. He was right: they were good. By the time I finished the whole stack, I liked the man who wrote them very much.

20

plucking chickens

Four months later, newly affianced to the man named Schuyler, I am sitting just past dark in a backyard in the flats of Oakland, holding a dead chicken between my spread knees and concentrating hard. Pinfeathers are fine and require a pincer grip. After they're killed, the chickens are plunged into buckets of hot water to loosen the feathers and the cuticle of the feet. This December evening, the water cools fast. My fingertips are puckered from the moisture, my knuckles a little stiff from the cold. I have never seen these people, mostly black, before tonight, nor have I ever plucked a chicken, but I feel oddly comfortable here, as if I've found my way back to a home I'd long forgotten.

We sit in a circle, at least a dozen of us, on assorted lawn chairs, with several five-gallon white plastic detergent tubs full of water and a few smaller dishtubs full of birds in the center. Light spills into the yard from the windows of the house, and someone has moved an old floorlamp outside to help us see. Schuyler is elsewhere, on butcher detail, cutting up plucked birds.

The yard is crudely terraced. Below the level where we sit is another, given over to animal pens and a dusty herb garden. Here and there, collections of objects I recognize as sacred by the care someone has taken to arrange them dot the yard. Is it performance anxiety or some kind of weird competitiveness that makes me glance around the circle now and then to see how well or poorly other people work? A couple of the women are excellent pluckers, fast and sure-fingered. Most everybody else is either lazy or struggling. I figure I'm doing okay.

The best pluckers are the best talkers, too, which stands to reason—they've had time to learn the task and get to know each other
well. One woman says her car broke down last week and she can't afford to get it fixed just yet. The fastest plucker, I think her name is
Tina, says she takes the bus to work.

"I was so tired Monday night I fell asleep on the bus on the way
home," she says.

Besides laughing at various chicken jokes, this is the first topic
I've been able to contribute to. "I always sleep on the bus home," I
say. "I get on and pass out."

Tina rolls her eyes. "Around here, you doze off, you wake up
without your purse. It sure must be different where you live."

"I guess," I say. "I always hug my purse tight when I close my eyes."

Tina grins at me. Talk subsides for a while. My first chicken is
naked as a baby. I hold it up by the feet, looking for feathers I may
have missed. From across the circle, Tina peers at my bird. "You sure
did a good job on that chicken's asshole, girl," she says.

"Thanks," I say. "I think I'm done with this one."

An Hispanic-looking woman, her square face framed by a white
bandana, regards my chicken critically. "You gotta peel the feet," she
says, with the lilt of a Latin accent. Everyone groans. I confess I don't
know how. I'm grateful to the others who say they don't, either. The
bandana woman shows us: slit the chitinous coating with your
thumbnail, then peel it away, taking care to clean it all the way down
to the claws. It takes me quite a while to get the feet done perfectly.
When I put my first chicken with a batch of others on the tray, I feel
absurdly proud of myself. I'm about to reach into the bucket for bird
number two when Tina says, "Hey, how about you do the asshole on
this one, too? I hate those tough little feathers down there."

So I have a specialty. "Give it to Doctor Anus," I say, and Tina
hands me the bird. When the chicken butt is bald and bare, I smoke
half a cigarette, then reach into the bucket for my next bird. What I

pull out is a soft gray dove. With a little imagination, you can under-stand the ancestral relationship between poultry and dinosaurs; you can see why the chicken is not king of the beasts, but a dove is a work of art, a bird drawn on the world's surface with just a few spare graceful curves. The force of pluck that pulls a chicken feather free is enough to tear the soft gray/pink skin of the dove. This is an exercise in tender restraint, a concentration so focused that while I pluck the dove, I'm all but oblivious to everything else around me.

After the soft small body is clean, I start on the dove's severed head. On each side of it, an eye as lustrous as a black pearl even in death regards me with mild fixity, no evident emotion. This is close and careful work, and as I gently tease feathers out of flesh, underly-ing form is revealed, the fine bones of the bird's skull, the seamless juncture of beak and skin, an organism halfway between life's confu-sions and the formal reduction of death. I find I am hardly breathing as I pluck. When I'm done, I hold the fine thing on my palm for a moment, knowing it is at least as beautiful as it is strange. I say a little prayer—to the dove? to the force that designed the dove?—then set it on the tray among the other birds.

When one of the priests comes to collect the tray, she looks the birds over, then picks up the dove's head. She smiles faintly and tosses it in the garbage can where we deposit our feathers. "We don't use that part," she tells the group at large. "You don't have to pull the feathers off."

Tina sends me a look of commiseration, and somebody else says, "*Now* they tell us." For a moment, people wait for my reaction.

My reaction is to laugh. I have spent a long time making some-thing lovely of no possible use. This seems to me to be a perfect para-ble about the nature of art, how it is futile and necessary at the same time.

It's cold enough outside now that my laughter shows up as steam. I take another chicken from the bucket and begin to pluck.

21

attractors

It was clear from the start that Schuyler was different.

He followed up our first date with an invitation to dine with several of his closest women friends. In order to feel less singular, I invited my daughter, then sixteen and always an astute judge of character, to come along. The parties sniffed and circled, discovered people and experiences in common. For a brief stolen moment, Schuyler and I sat quietly on the front-porch steps and smoked. My daughter liked him, with reservations. After our third date, cheap Vietnamese noodles and a long walk with Cecil B. DeMille lighting diffuse over Puget Sound affirming the grace of God, he kissed my cheek. On the fourth, in the mountains with our boy-children, we succumbed to curiosity and surrendered our virtue into one another's keeping. Finally, he invited me into his sanctum sanctorum. Against one wall of his writer's office, he had created an altar for his ancestors. In their photos, they were a stern and mostly handsome bunch of WASPy eastern Washington settlers, merchants, dentists, whose eyes regarded me with unsmiling speculation when Schuyler introduced us.

He called the altar a boveda. It was covered with white cloth, lighted by white candles. White flowers blossomed in a clear vase. A clear glass bowl held water. On one corner of the table, a single white blossom floated in a glass of water. A small white cup held golden honey.

"I put that there to attract you," Schuyler said.

I asked him to explain.

Some months before, in the course of performing a misa blanca for him, Rosi, partner of Maria, a gifted medium and priest of Eleggua, had seen a woman with two children, a boy and a girl, coming toward him. Rosi had told him the relative ages of the children and added that he would be an important force in the life of the boy. She had told him he would experience both spiritual connection and sexual pleasure with the woman such as he'd never known before. The woman, Rosi had told him, would reveal nothing more about herself. She would not give her name. But the honey would draw her to him. If he put it on his altar, she would come.

"I guess it worked," he said, with a smile that might have melted diamonds. "Here you are."

22

my first bembe

The day after I plucked my first chicken, I attended my first bembe. Schuyler was still very young in the religion then, but compared to me, he was an elder. What did I know? That good manners required me to dress in white and cover my head. That I should have a few loose dollars tucked away in easy reach, to pay the drummers, to give away as needed. That I was going to a party which assorted orishas might also attend. I remember being nervous and excited, hoping I would be welcome, praying I would not do something stupid and thereby give offence. I don't remember approaching any other religious ceremony with the hope, the fear, the titillating promise that I might come face-to-face with tangible, living, breathing avatars of God.

The house in Oakland held its sacred rites and parties in the detached garage, an outbuilding that, put to conventional uses, might have accommodated two cars and a small shop. That day, there was an elaborate altar in one corner, a seated drum ensemble, and upwards of fifty people pressed into the space. With a few notable, deliberate exceptions, everyone wore white, and they wore it variously. There was a contingent of handsome black and light brown women who wore billowing white skirts over lacy white pantaloons, whose heads were wrapped in towering white turbans, whose jewelry was bold and plentiful. These women knew all the words to all the songs, the steps to all the dances, they knew the shape of the ritual, and they knew each other. Among them, younger, slimmer, more boyish women adapted the white rule to their natural styles—white jeans, white sweat pants, white overalls, white suits or skirts or dresses—clothing of more contemporary fashion that happened to be white instead of existing to be white. It was at foot level that the whiteness became dilute, giving way to athletic shoes, white save for Nike swooshes, or to dark leather. The men, fewer in number, seemed more haphazard in their white dressing, although a male minority was beautifully, elegantly clad.

At the bembe that day, there were no very old people and only a handful of children and teenagers. We, in our mid-forties, were just outside the major twentysomething-to-forty demographic bulge. No prayer books, no hymnals, no mimeographed order of service mapped the proceedings. Half a dozen folding chairs against one wall offered respite to the footsore. It was very close in the garage.

When we first entered, the company stood at relaxed though reverent attention, facing the drummers and listening to the drums. It was nearly impossible to keep the voices of the drums from sounding in the body, but during this first instrumental interlude, no one danced; people just swayed or shuffled a bit in time. After maybe half an hour of drumming, there was a small intermission, a chance for people to prostrate themselves on a grass mat in front of the altar to pray, and before one another, according to a hierarchy based on age in the religion, not in the world. Upon rising, people crossed their arms over their chests and bumped shoulders, diagonally, right to right, left to left. The salutes ended in hugs. When Schuyler and I slipped outside to share a cigarette, it was winter in the yard, drizzly and chill. Inside the garage, it was July.

Some mysterious signal called everyone back from the intermission. Earlier in the day, when we first arrived at the house, a grandmotherly woman in a faded housecoat and curlers had slumped at the kitchen table, chatting with Maria and Rosi in fast Spanish, interrupting herself only long enough for her to draw on the cigarette in her right hand or the mug of coffee in her left. Now that same woman stood next to the drummers in spike heels, twenty years younger or maybe ageless, shapely in a big-shouldered, fitted turquoise suit, her coarse, still mostly dark hair billowing about her shoulders. Lips and fingernails red. Rhinestones flashing from her spectacles and in her ears. Brashly sexy, with the honeyed self-assurance, the wide-legged front-and-center stance of Lauren Bacall once she had a couple of Bogart movies under her belt and a drink in her hand. This was the singer. This was Estelle.

You could hear the smoking in her voice, but the texture in the top notes only added to its authority. The three double-headed drums, as graduated in size as the three bears, as wasp-waisted as Estelle in her silk suit, sang with and around her, not so much percussion as a trio with a beat. When Estelle called, the company answered her in beautiful shards of a language I know now is Lucumi. With the singing, the dancing began. That mass of bodies synchronized itself into a motion as fluid and undulant as the roll of the sea. While the ritual couldn't wash away my ignorance of the tradition, still it gathered me up and floated me along, mouthing something like the words, moving my feet in something like the steps the people around me were doing. When I glanced at Schuyler, who'd drifted a bit away in the flow of the crowd, his attention, too, was trained on Estelle; he, too, was doing a reasonable job of faking it.

Faking and not. I don't know the map of my own consciousness in clinical detail, brain function matched to anatomy, but I do know that the music and the dance of the tambour understood my central nervous system very well indeed, at a level of sophistication I'd never quite experienced before. I didn't know what our common purpose was, but I understood that we *had* one as we sang and danced; even in my ignorance, I shared the urgency and the will of the group. After a while, I began to sense that we collectively were an instrument, that Estelle played us with her voice. The temperature in the garage rose still further with the intensity of our desire. We had tremendous power and yet were finely tuned.

Suddenly, in unison, the whole company squatted down, touching the floor with the fingers of one hand. Estelle was addressing her song with great insistence to just one youngish man in blue. He staggered as if he were drunk, and his eyes were wild, like the eyes of a cornered animal. As the singer remonstrated with him, a couple of priests of the house appeared on either side of the young man. They took him into what looked like protective custody. A corridor opened through the crowd, and the priests escorted the young man out of the garage. As soon as he was gone, the company stood up again, and after a beat or two of transition, the ceremony recommenced. Schuyler found his way back to my side and spoke low into my ear.

"Orisha is here," is what he said.

My former husband had made an award-winning TV documentary on religion in America. It included a segment about a group of evangelicals in the American South who spoke in tongues and handled snakes. His footage, and his stories of filming it, were all I knew of trance possession. In the context of the Christians in his film, it looked out of control, messy, and dangerous—plump sweaty men in shirt sleeves, middle-aged ladies in flowered dresses reeling about in quasi-sexual ecstasy, each on a separate self-involved trip, in a many-ringed circus that had no master except hysteria. What happened in the garage in Oakland could not have been more different.

Drumming, singing, and dancing invited orishas to attend the party. When a priest began to go into trance, Estelle was immediately attuned, singing him or her safely through the mystery. Godsisters and -brothers of the priest being ridden stayed close, offering physical and psychic protection, refreshment, and hospitality. The visiting orishas had come in order to address members of the house with advice and warnings, to cleanse them, to celebrate with them, or to dispense blessings. Because some of the orishas who came down spoke only Spanish, a bilingual priest stayed close to their side, translating messages instantly. If someone who was new to trance fell prey to the ritual and began to go under, he or she was gently but firmly guided from the room and brought around outside.

Because I sometimes taught workshops, gave speeches or readings, I had some understanding of what it is to manage the energies of a group of diverse people. Estelle's sense of the room and her ability to manipulate it, her commitment to keeping everyone in it safe, was amazing—intelligence and intuition working in tandem with a finesse I'd never seen in action before. It was only later that I learned something about the third leg of that stool: the vast amount of sheer information about the religion, processed on the fly, that informs the gifts of an effective singer, an akpuon.

Drums, songs, dances. Not just *any* drums, songs, dances, but *these* drums, *these* songs and dances, born countless centuries before in Africa, carried with bold and loving secrecy to a new continent, disguised and protected against the degradations of slavery, passed soul to soul, laboriously, in long apprenticeships—drums, songs, and dances that formed a bridge between human and divine. That day for the first time I saw the bridge built, and I saw it carry traffic back and forth. I could see that the bridge was sturdy and artfully made. I could see that it was carefully maintained. I could see all this despite whatever baggage of personal disappointment, liberal education, and inherited doubt I carried with me to the bembe that day. Any clever attempts to explain away what I witnessed and what I felt died of their own smug weight. I stayed to the rear of the dancers and did my best to copy the movements of the women in front of me. I added my voice to the songs. My whole being was filled with wonder, and inside my ears I could hear the song my blood was singing: *This is it, this is it, this is it.*

That was six years ago.

• • •

At least four orishas showed up at the bembe that Sunday afternoon. Estelle had her hands full, bringing them down and looking after them once they arrived. Yemolla was motherly and stern, with a tendency to bark like a seal; Ochun was a golden cat licking honey from a plate; Obatala was old, frail, sweet, and rather shy. They mixed with the company, sometimes dancing, sometimes stopping to chat. Not all their interactions were serious, by any means. They could be playful, impious, and wonderfully loving, too. I watched them all closely, and whatever cynical desire I had to bust them as actors soon gave way to a sense of utter delight at being in their presence. The last to arrive at the party was Maria's Oggun.

I am quite convinced no dancer or actor could emulate the transformation that takes place when Oggun rides Maria. Her Oggun is fierce, powerful, loud, and abrasive. His movements are huge and full of crude grace. He is wild-eyed and humorless, hotheaded, and beneath the cigar-chomping swagger, as forthright as a child. Anything put in his hands, he takes for a machete and uses to slice his way through the room, blazing trail. Oggun the archetype is a tireless worker, and when Oggun arrives in a room, it is as raw energy, a locomotive steaming full tilt up the tracks. Maria's Oggun is pretty scary, as I soon had occasion to learn.

As the bembe unfolded around us, Schuyler and I got separated in the throng. I was still in my refuge by the back wall; he'd moved toward the center of the room in order to salute Oggun. He was the only person I knew there, and I was newly in love with him, so I tried to keep him in my peripheral vision all the time. I watched as he prostrated before the warrior in his grass skirt, watched as Oggun yanked him sharply to his feet and started to pound on Schuyler's chest with the heel of his hand. The recoil each strike produced proved the blows were not pretend. Even above the drumming, I could hear Oggun declaiming loudly in Spanish.

After a little while, Rosi found Schuyler and Oggun in the crowd and started to translate Oggun's message to Schuyler. I was, of course, intensely curious about what was being said. The harangue went on a few minutes more, then Oggun gave Schuyler a hard shove and spun away from him. Hunched forward with a hunter's alertness, he scanned the crowd. When his fierce eyes found me, Oggun strode forward, not stopping until he was close enough to reach out and grab me firmly by the wrist. He said nothing but pulled me along after him, back to Schuyler and Rosi in the middle of the crowd.

When we got there, Oggun started shouting at Schuyler again, pounding on his shoulder, with Rosi translating as quickly as she could.

"Oggun says Ochun sent you her daughter. You see? And you have to take care of her, and love her, and love Ochun, or . . ."

I didn't get to hear the or-clause, because at that point, Oggun let go of my wrist and shoved me backward, away from him. I traveled quite a distance on the force of that launch, staggering, bounced off surrounding bodies.

By the time I made my way back to Schuyler's side, Oggun was gone and Schuyler was weeping softly, deeply moved by the attention of the orisha. To him, Oggun's message meant he was beloved. I was of two minds—glad to have such a tough protector, warning my new fiancé to treat me right, and bemused that someone or something else took credit for our romance.

Who was this Ochun, to call me her daughter?

23

Harriet & the geriatric specialist

My mother eventually did make a friend at the Grosvenor House. Harriet was the third and last wife of a local funeral home magnate, the wife he'd married purely for pleasure's sake. Before she met him, she'd worked retail in an exclusive downtown department store. Now, a rich widow, she shopped there. Harriet had a salty tongue, a sense of humor, and a lot of stories, which may have been what endeared her to my mother. Their camaraderie featured at least a couple of martini-studded evenings a week in the cocktail lounge off the lobby, after-dinner Drambuies in one another's digs, and a real solicitude for one another's aches and pains. When Harriet first met us, my mother's family, she came armed with helium balloons. Within minutes, she and my kids and I were bouncing off the walls in a no-holds-barred game of helium soccer that we made up as we went along. My mother pretended to disapprove of our antics, but I could tell she liked the giddiness. Our phone conversations during those days were peppered with sentences that started out "Harriet and I" or "Harriet says," and it seemed as if life finally had a flavor that piqued my mother's appetite.

Then Harriet was hospitalized for GI surgery. Almost as soon as she got home, she had a stroke that left her paralyzed on one side and wheelchair bound. Her round-the-clock private nurses were brusque and professional, under orders to hide the smokes and keep the martinis to a minimum. My mother had the time and the inclination to be a good friend, I think, but the nurses were so efficient at their designated tasks that there wasn't much left for an amateur to do. Once after Harriet's stroke I invited her to join me and my mom for drinks and dinner at the Grove. She was delivered to our table by a starched white attendant, and even though I assured the woman I'd return Harriet, wheelchair and all, to her apartment a couple of hours hence, the LPN insisted on sitting at a nearby table nursing a solitary bottomless glass of house white and watching us while we ate. The surveillance, coupled with the difficulty Harriet had speaking, put a damper on the evening.

Harriet declined rapidly after that. Losing the companionship she'd so lately found made my mother's isolation seem twice as deep as it had been before. Now she began to phone-order groceries from the nearby QFC—gourmet frozen dinners, nondairy creamer, canned soups, toaster crumpets, ice-cream, and butterhorns—and to go to the dining room less and less often. I took to bringing her what amounted to health food—fruits, vegetables, yogurt, meat, and cheese—to offset the carbohydrates and chemicals she ordered up herself. These festered in the refrigerator, while my mom got plumper and plumper, with less and less muscle on her frame. Her primary exercise consisted of frequent trips from her television-watching chair to the bathroom and back. It didn't take a professional to figure out she was depressed.

It's an inborn kink of the Scandinavian psyche that while depression is almost commonplace, seeking help for it is as exotic and distasteful an idea as serving raw parrot with habanero peppers for breakfast. My timid attempts to suggest it might be possible to change things were met with wounded silence or scathing disdain. Is it possible to help somebody who wants no part of your assistance? Do we have a moral obligation to persist in the face of rejection? These were questions that haunted me through the early '90s. I learned about myself that I am either incurably optimistic or vastly stubborn. When direct suggestion failed to produce the desired results, I resorted to stealth and sneakery.

My mother was a patient of the Polyclinic, a Seattle healthcare organization conceived in the 1970s that gathered dozens and dozens of general practitioners and specialists together under the same roof, the same business plan, and the same billing service. It was supposed to provide virtues of proximity and economies of scale for all concerned. My parents followed their GP into this huge group practice. When he retired, they were passed on to another doctor they didn't much like, with the result that, while my mother had an oncologist for her breast cancer and a cardiologist for her heart disease, there really was no one physician playing with a full deck. Opining that someone ought to look at the whole picture and figure out if the cabinet full of medications my mom was taking for her various conditions were necessary and safe in combination, I proposed we find her a new doctor. My mom agreed. The doctor I selected was the only one the Polyclinic called a geriatric specialist back then. The clerk who made the appointments assured me that Dr. X was "wonderful."

No more than five seconds into his acquaintance with my mother, Dr. X had excited her antagonism. Number one, he was short. Number two, he was foreign. Number three, he was what my father would have called "a Christer," this evident from the beaming Jesus and the calligraphed homilies on his walls. Four, he was over-bearingly cheerful. Five, he talked down to my mother. Number six, he assumed she actually wanted his help.

When he led with, "Hello there, Mrs. Thompson; I understand we've been feeling blue," I knew we were in trouble. My mother's back went straight up. When he asked her if she missed my father, she informed him that this was not a matter of medical concern. Dr. X tried to explain that emotional causes could manifest themselves as physical effects. He inquired about her social life. He asked if she did any volunteer work. Was she the member of a church? How often did she get out of the house? In each case, and with growing irritation, my mother responded that taking care of her body might be his job but the state of her soul was none of his business.

The doctor was flummoxed. He was a nice enough man, he had considerable charm and a righteous shtick, and he clearly wasn't used to being stonewalled. Whenever he thought my mother wouldn't catch him at it, he rolled his eyes at me. Hard case.

You betcha, Doc.

Finally, he said, "Mrs. Thompson, I know your daughter has some concerns about your lifestyle and your emotional wellbeing. Why don't we ask her to share those with us now?"

There was no way to let him know what I'd already figured out—that he was not the right third party to help us have the conversation we couldn't seem to sustain by ourselves. If he couldn't see that using the verb "to share" in reference to any act of communion more intimate than splitting a restaurant check or a piece of chocolate pie was a serious mistake, well, there wasn't much hope for a transformational outcome here. Still, I tried.

"Mom, I'm really concerned that you never leave your apartment. I know how much you wanted to live downtown, but if you don't take advantage of being there, I don't see that there's much point. The kids and I would really like you to move into the condo two doors down from us so we can see you every day."

"Familiarity breeds contempt." My mother's voice was icy.

"You'd still have your own home. You'd just have family close by. You'd have company every day. And I'm not a bad cook."

"You live in a backwater. There's nothing there for me," she said.

"You never leave your apartment. If you lived by us, you could get out every day."

"Don't do this, Joyce," my mother said.

"I have to, Mom. I have to because I love you. And I want you to understand that your grandchildren and I want to be part of your life. We want to know you and enjoy you and help you out."

Dr. X cleared his throat. "Uh, Mrs. Thompson, it seems to me that your daughter and her family are making you a sincere and generous offer here. Most of my patients would be thrilled if their children wanted them nearby."

"I'm not most of your patients," my mother said. She turned to me. "This is all very well now. But two years from now I could be bedridden. Or you could want to move."

"And we'd find the right solution then. We would have had two good years."

My mother shook her head. "No, Joyce. You don't understand. I don't want to talk about this anymore."

By now the doctor was depressed. Consulting his watch, he saw that the twelve minutes allotted to us had elapsed. "Look at that," he said. "I'm afraid we've run out of time. If you'd like to make an appointment with my nurse, she can schedule you for a complete physical. We can have a look at your medications then."

"I don't think we'll be coming back," my mother informed him, on our way out the door. When it closed behind us, the first thing she said was, "I need to go to the little girls' room." The second thing was, "That was for the birds. I didn't like him very much. Did you?"

24

red flags waving

In the ten years of my single-motherhood, the minimum acceptable distance from a lover's front doorstep to my own was about five hundred miles. My life with my children, the one in which I looked after my widowed mother, did not overlap with romance. My sex life was less physically than postally satisfying. It was a time highlighted by several intense correspondences, a couple of which grew into published works of poetry or prose. My reluctance to domesticate my paramours made it possible for me to know well several men who for one reason or another fell far outside the envelope meant to enclose a mate, and for these adventures, I will always be grateful. After ten years of my unsullied attention, all of my dependents, children and mother alike, were used to having *all* of me, absent the most occasional lost weekend, all to themselves. The sudden arrival of Schuyler, who inhabited the same area code, unsettled our established ways. I would like to say that no one suffered from the changes that ensued, but I doubt my children would let me get by with it. Change is hard, even when it is not perceived as loss.

Quantitatively, I probably spent the same number of hours per week with and on behalf of my mother as before, but I was no doubt more perfunctory, less present than she was used to having me be. At least part of the time, Schuyler, too, was on hand. Schuyler finds flirting to be an important social art, and with my mother, he used it to advantage. Her own saucy side emerged in response to his, brightening her eyes, putting some unaccustomed color in her cheeks. They laughed together. It was clear that, whether or not she liked my having a local suitor, she did like *him*. That she never actually called him by name but always referred to him as "that fellow you see, what's his name" I took as a sly expression of her ambivalence at sharing my affections. It was one of several flags I was slow to recognize as red.

Saturday in spring, a day spent doing my mother's business. I recall it as a hard day, one of those combustible days when the differences between our natures seemed irreconcilable and peace was always in danger of going south fast, a day on which I would, if asked, have counseled against the making of deathbed promises.

I'm sure my mother is as tired and as out of sorts as I am by the time we pull into the bank parking lot to discharge the last of our errands. Just half an hour more and I'll be on a ferryboat back to my family. My mother will be alone. I feel guilty enough about this that I am determined to hold on to my composure at all costs, to help the day end kindly.

I kill the engine and unloose my mother's seatbelt. She turns in her seat to face me. "I've been meaning to tell you," she says. "I think that your young Ian is getting a little big for his britches."

If you want to get on my bad side quickly, go ahead, speak ill of my children. I choke back the first surge of adrenaline. "What do you mean?" I ask. How unnaturally level my voice is. I wonder if my mother notices.

"He holds the floor longer than a youngster has any right to," my mother says. "It's not seemly."

"Seemly," I mutter.

"I'm not saying children should be seen and not heard, you understand," my mother says. "But your young man should definitely be heard a good deal less, in my humble opinion."

As always, I am tempted to tell my mother that there's nothing the least bit humble about her opinion. Instead, I choose words carefully. "He *is* full of opinions," I say. "But they're usually opinions on the subject at hand."

"Still, he's a showoff," my mother says. "You need to rein him in."

"He has a lively mind," I say. "He listens to other people. When he goes on too long, I kick him under the table."

"You should kick him more often, then," my mother says.

For a moment, my hand hovers over the detonator. For a moment, I am willing to start the unwinnable war. Then I pull back. Change direction. "Aw, come on," I say. "You can hardly blame him for having inherited the family gift of gab." The words are conciliatory, even if my voice now sounds a little shrill. "Maybe he'll grow up to be a lawyer like you."

In an instant, my mother's expression softens and she steps into a different space—not the close quarters of my Ford Escort, where tempers can grow short, but the psychic stage from which she tells her stories. It is her safe place. In it, she has confidence and charm.

"It was the fall of my sophomore year in college," my mother says, "and I was enrolled in Professor Hornsby's elocution class. I was taking it as part of my drama major, but in the fall it was one of the classes the football team always took, the best players and the worst students, because it was Professor Hornsby's policy to give nothing lower than a C-minus to a member of the varsity football squad, no matter how poor a speaker.

"Everyone else in the class, mind you, was expected to toe the line. Well, as luck would have it, I was expected to deliver my first recitation on the day of the big game against UCLA. All of the football players in the class were feeling their oats. Maybe they were taking something, for all I know. I was nervous enough about having to stand up in front of the class and declaim, but that day all these big bohunks were sitting together in the last row, and they couldn't be quiet or sit still to save their lives.

"I was supposed to deliver Portia's speech about the quality of

mercy from *The Merchant of Venice,* and Professor Hornsby told the
boys they couldn't leave for the game until they'd had their daily dose
of culture. They hooted and chortled and misbehaved through my
whole performance. When I was done, the professor told them that
if they won against the Bruins, they would owe their victory to
William Shakespeare and Miss Anna Olson. I'm sure it took me all
weekend to stop blushing," my mother says.

It's quite a long story, and by the time she's done telling it, my
mother is relaxed and smiling. I'm less tense myself. It's not a story
from her current collection; if I've ever heard it, it was years and
years ago. "So tell me," I say, "did the Huskies win the game?"

For as long as it takes for one heartbeat to follow on the last one,
my mother looks at me. Then she blinks, straightens her shoulders,
cocks her head just slightly to the left. "It was the fall of my sophomore year in college," my mother says, "and I was enrolled in Professor Hornsby's elocution class. I was taking it as part of my drama
major, but in the fall it was one of the classes the football team always took, the best players and the worst students, because it was
Professor Hornsby's policy to give nothing lower than a C-minus to a
member of the varsity football squad, no matter how poor a speaker.

"Everyone else in the class, mind you, was expected to toe the
line. Well, as luck would have it, I was expected to deliver my first
recitation on the day of the big game against UCLA. All of the football
players in the class were feeling their oats. Maybe they were taking
something, for all I know. I was nervous enough about having to
stand up in front of the class and declaim, but that day all these big
bohunks were sitting together in the last row, and they couldn't be
quiet or sit still to save their lives.

"I was supposed to deliver Portia's speech about the quality of
mercy from *The Merchant of Venice,* and Professor Hornsby told the
boys they couldn't leave for the game until they'd had their daily dose
of culture. They hooted and chortled and misbehaved through my

whole performance. When I was done, the professor told them that if they won against the Bruins, they would owe their victory to William Shakespeare and Miss Anna Olson. I'm sure it took me all weekend to stop blushing," my mother says.

"What a good story," I make myself say when she finishes. "Who won the game?"

And my mother says, "Why are we sitting here? Have we done the banking yet or not?"

She really doesn't know.

three stories about Ochun

sailing my shoe to Timbuktu

In child memories, focus is immediate, tight, bound to the senses. Try as I might, I can't zoom in on the vegetation, so I have to read the season by the color of the light. Even though it's hot, the light is lemony. In August it would be butterscotch. So this must be May. In the orchard, the flowers have fallen from the apple trees. The ones that got pollinated by bees or breeze are busily becoming fruit. On the ground, the brief white blossoms have turned brown. The cows have the run of the place, grazing among wizened trunks scabbed with lichen. Beyond the boundaries of the orchard, in the woods, the trilliums and bleeding hearts have pushed up out of leaf mold to declare full spring. The end of every branch of every evergreen is pale green, new growth soft as a puppy's fur.

A creek runs through these woods, and in May it is spring-giddy, the water high and sparkling, noisy among the stones. My Uncle Emmett and I kneel beside it. We are making boats from leaves and twigs, launching them into the current, bound for Mukilteo and Timbuktu. I have no idea where these places are, but I love saying their names. From Leaf Creek to the Cedar River, from Cedar River to the sea, our boats sail, and we agree, my uncle and I, that their cargo is important. Sometimes it is messages, sometimes spices, sometimes emeralds and rubies. Sometimes it is watermelons. Sometimes it is lambs.

My Uncle Emmett is the only grownup I know who has a fully functioning imagination. We both believe in our boats. We are both barefoot in the creekbed, the rolled-up cuffs of our trousers long since soaked. We are laughing, and so is the little stream. My mother isn't here with us, and I don't know why.

If I look back over forty-plus years, though, I can figure it out. If I am four, and I believe I am, then my mother's mother is still alive. She has already had a stroke or two and spends most of her time in bed. I really don't remember her before the strokes. In fact, I have exactly one memory of her alive. I stand by her bed, as still as I can be, and hold her crooked old hand. She calls me her pet, her jewel, which makes me wonder if she knows my name. She doesn't die until my sixth birthday, the very day. My mother must be with her mother now, sitting beside her brass bed, while Emmett and I play in the creek.

My Uncle Emmett is my mother's favorite of her five brothers. He was seventeen years old when she was born. For a good piece of her growing up, he was away, conscripted in wars or seeing the world. He spent some time in Panama, working on the canal. He went to automobile school in San Francisco, learning everything there was to know about those new machines. In the old pictures, he is handsome and a bit of a dandy, with a cocky, heart-melting grin. Once he came home to Maple Valley and made her acquaintance, his little sister Anne adored him. I don't believe she ever stopped.

Now he rocks back on his heels and sits down on the bank, his bare feet still in the creek, and pulls out his red can of Prince Albert and his rolling papers. Time for a smoke. Now instead of being with my uncle in the creek, I am with the creek. Instead of hearing his voice laughing, I hear the voice of the water. It's cool and clear and very pure, that sound. The creek is in a very good mood. I spread my hands out on the rocks of the creekbed. The sun shines through the water on them, so they look very white, and the movement of the water creates fast-moving shadows that dart across them, like fish that are visible but have no mass. Does that make them ghost fish? Soon I am humming the creek's song. I want to be a twig-boat with a leaf mast and sail away to Mukilteo and Timbuktu.

If I did, my mother would be angry at my uncle for letting me go.

Instead of going myself, it occurs to me that I can send my shoe. My shoe is a Keds canvas Mary Jane, with a strap and a buckle. It is blue and it is new and I like it very much. But the fact is, I have two of them. I climb out of the water long enough to pick a handful of wildflowers. I put them in my blue shoe. I tell my shoe it is going on an important journey. I am happy inside. In the creek, I hold my shoe-boat in the current and sing a little song about Mukilteo and Timbuktu.

From the bank, my Uncle Emmett asks me what I'm doing, and I tell him my shoe is a boat. I am sending it downstream to the sea.

Mischief dances in his eyes like sunshine dances on the water. "Go ahead, then," he says, and leans back on his elbows on the bank, to enjoy the show.

Where the water is deepest, I entrust my shoe to the stream. It bobs and bounces away, nudging against obstacles, then nosing around them. Downstream, the creek bends to the left and then I can see my boat no more. My heart pounds to watch it disappear. As if from a great distance, I hear my uncle laughing and the water laughing and a silly, silvery little sound that must be me laughing, too.

When my mother comes, my uncle tells her proudly that we have sent my left blue shoe to Mukilteo and Timbuktu. I will either have to hop on one foot back to the big house, or he will have to carry me.

My mother doesn't get mad at us. She laughs. My Uncle Emmett scoops me up in his arms.

I am four years old, and I have just made my first offering to Ochun.

seduction by language

At church camp the summer I am eleven, I fall in love with Father Mills. Since it is an Episcopal church camp, he is under no obligation of celibacy, so I assume that loving him is not a sin. Father Mills is the youngest of the clergy on the camp staff, just barely out of seminary, and the only one who isn't married. To tell you the truth, he isn't very attractive physically, being extremely pale and rather plump, with hair and plastic glasses' frames as black as the short-sleeve minister shirts he wears no matter how hot it gets. Why would an eleven-year-old girl fall in love with him, when there are so many lean, tan, athletic thirteen- and fourteen-year-old boys at camp?

To tell you more truth, although I am absolutely confident that all this will change one day, I am presently not all that attractive myself. I have glasses and braces and a crummy haircut. I, too, am pale. Besides, even though my body has been on the planet just over a decade, I seem to have an old soul. This is something I have known about myself for most of my young life. It means I would rather read poems than play softball. I would rather meet Jesus than Jerry Lee Lewis. Until I fell in love with Father Mills, my most romantic fantasy had to do with becoming a nun, although with the onset of puberty and the discovery of a particular flowering feeling I seem able to produce pretty much at will by squeezing my thigh muscles together in just the right way, the convent is rapidly losing ground as a career path. To be the wife of a holy man seems a promising alternative.

From a combination of intuition and observation, I have concluded that Father Mills has soul. He keeps his eyes tightly closed when he prays. He crosses himself often, suggesting diligent piety. Even when he is on lifeguard duty at the camp pool, he reads, nothing trashy. I have never caught him looking at the older girls in their two-piece bathing suits the way all the other males in the camp do, including the ministers. He has a wonderful vocabulary, with an endless supply of large, Latin-sounding words.

Ilse, the head camp counselor, is twenty-one years old and slender, with a quiet dignity. I can tell she, too, is attracted to Father Mills. Because they're both on staff, she has many more chances to ply her suit than I do. He seems wary but pleased by her attentions.

How to compete?

Every afternoon, the whole camp observes, or is supposed to observe, a whole hour of silent meditation. A lot of the older campers take to their bunks and snooze. Some sunbathe silently beside the pool. The cool bad kids hike up the trail behind the camp, smoke cigarettes, and whisper dirty jokes. A few pious losers sit in the outdoor chapel and pray or read the Bible, something I might do myself except for the social stigma and the mosquitoes. The most beautiful of the girls go to the river that runs along the eastern edge of the camp, sit on the flat hot rocks, and wash their hair.

One day, I take my lovesick heart to the river.

I settle in upstream of the hairwashers, on a little patch of sand among the rocks. Our camp is in the mountains, and the river is near its source, cold and forceful, thirty feet across from bank to bank, shallow at the verges, deep in the channel. Its voice is not so much a song as a powerful exhalation, a steady outpouring of breath from, from . . . the lungs of God! That's it. Or should it be the lips?

I listen again, harder. As if it were a musical chord, the river sound is made up of several different but concurrent notes.

Good word, *concurrent*—sounds grown up.

There's the pure rush, true, but there's also the hiss it makes when a big rock parts it up the middle, and a kind of tinkle on the top. Above that, above the water, the wind is talking in the trees. If I listen really hard, I can convince myself the different kinds of trees have different voices, depending on the shape and density of their foliage. I can hear what they're saying. The trees are talking about love, but I don't actually write that down. Instead I choose to say they're praying. It's practically the same thing, right?

Just to make sure I've got it nailed, I close my eyes. The river song surrounds me, as completely as if I were inside a cocoon of sound, in a womb. I feel something rise up out of the very center of my chest and yearn toward the river, join in its long flight down to the sea.

Holy moly, could that be my soul?

The thought is so alarming I have to open my eyes, get my bearings. Feeling a little dizzy here. Feeling a little bit transcendent.

Most eleven-year-olds don't know that word, but I do.

I lift my hand to push my bangs up off my face, and when I do, I find that my forehead and my hair are cool and damp, coated in river spray so fine I didn't feel it land. I run my finger across my cheek contemplatively, feeling the cool moisture there, and the soft fuzz. I feel the way my cheek changes when I start to smile.

I am smiling because now, suddenly, I know how I am going to get Father Mills's attention. I am going to write about the river. I am going to write about the river better than anyone he's ever known could possibly write about the river. I am going to write about the river and it is going to make him love me, not quite in the way a man loves a woman—that would be too much to ask—but love me nonetheless, the way one spirit loves another. He is going to find himself wishing that slender Ilse were more like me.

No, I have not taken leave of my senses. I have not lost my grip on reality. It doesn't work on everyone, of course—you have to have a certain sensibility, a certain sensitivity, a certain proclivity—but it's true and I know it. I am eleven and have already known this for two years.

With words it is possible to win love.

I submitted my meditation on the river to the camp newspaper anonymously. Father Mills was the editor, of course, and he read the day's work sitting beside the pool in a lounge chair right after lunch. I spread out my beach towel and pretended to sunbathe right where I could watch his face as he read. It was easy to tell when he came to my piece. First, his eyes opened wider. Then they started to move faster and faster across the page, gulping my words as if they were water and he was a very thirsty man. His jaw seemed to soften, and a faint smile appeared on his lips. He combed his hair with his fingers. He looked up and out, into the middle distance. Shook his head a little bit.

I got up then and wrapped my beach towel chastely around me, over my purple one-piece bathing suit. I slid my feet into my thongs. Ever so shyly, I approached Father Mills.

"Uh, excuse me. I put a . . . a meditation in your mailbox this morning. Only I think I forgot to put my name on it."

For the first time, Father Mills looked directly at me. For the first time, I was no longer an extra on the set called camp. "A meditation?" he said.

"About the river."

Oh, the look that came into his eyes, that amazement, that sweet appraisal. Game, set, match. On the spot, he made me his assistant editor. We worked closely together for what remained of the two-week session. Because I was working on the paper, I had a way out of the otherwise mandatory evening softball games and never had to be picked last again. Instead, we had many interesting discussions about life, and literature, and faith. Even skinny Ilse had to be nice to me.

I heard some time later that Ilse had gotten engaged to Father Mills. They may have gotten married, for all I know.

After summer camp, I never saw either one of them again. But I went to the river many more times.

a small real miracle

The Green, the Quilcene, the Fraser and the Thompson, the Sno-qualmie, the Ipswich, the Essex, the Dungeness, the Hudson, the Charles, Fall Creek Gorge, the Nehalem, the Skagit, the Dosewallips, the Columbia at Astoria, at Vantage. More, whose names I have forgotten, or never knew. Rivers. Holy places. Prayers, and all the secrets of my heart. Long before I heard of orisha, long before she had a name, I was a supplicant and devotee of Ochun. It was to her I whispered everything I wanted in a soulmate—that he should be smart and funny, pleasing to my eye, sensual, spiritual, a man with fast friends, a man who already knew how to love. A twice-born man. That the river heard and answered me is affirmed by the fact that Schuyler is everything I asked for.

Now it is August and I am forty-nine years old. Just past noon, the light is sweet and rich as caramel, the river busy and oh, so cold. This time it is the Tolt. Downstream there are fishermen, upstream kids swimming, twentysomethings floating on inner tubes and drinking beer. Now I know Ochun by name, know that she loves oranges, cinnamon, honey, brass; that yellow is her color, five her number; that she protects and saves her children, those whom she loves. Eros is her domain, and beauty, art, civilization. How can civilization rise where there is no river? It may be that she is a little vain, a bit too easily offended—high-maintenance, you might say—yet that's the prerogative of goddesses with skin the color of cloves, with flowing tresses, high breasts, and undulant curves, of women who smell like flowers, whose skin is smooth as silk and warm as summer wind, whose element is water, fresh, sweet, and never still. Fan-dancer, hip-swinger, Ochun is the queen of flirts. I am willing to believe she is my spiritual mother.

First, Schulyer and I ease our gifts into the water, all the things Ochun loves. Her frothy tongue licks honey from our white platter as quickly and neatly as a cat. One by one, we toss flowers into the water, peonies and mums, until yellow blossoms chart the down-stream current. The water is swift and cold against my calves. It feels delicious. With cupped hands, I wet my arms and face, pour water over my head. Schuyler stands in the river beside me, and for a moment we turn playful, splashing, trying to make each other lose footing on the slick rocks of the river-bottom. All this is stalling. We have come to the river to ask a gigantic favor.

I am terrified that Ochun will grant our request. I am equally terrified that she will not.

I'm addicted to the drug nicotine, and have been for thirty-five years—so long that neither my body nor my psyche remembers what it's like to live without it. I do know what it is like to try to quit. This I've done dozens, maybe hundreds of times, often enough that "craven" is my middle name. Failure is my familiar, "just this once" my mantra. Believe me, I have tried everything—hypnotism, beta-blockers, acupuncture, rationing, Nicorette gum, the patch, three times, prayer, the buddy system, tapering, and a whole flock of cold turkeys. Neither shame nor bribery nor threats of loss of love have held me fast. Always, always, I smoke my "last" cigarette and within a few hours or a few days light up my next. I am the woman who runs water into a fresh pack of cigarettes, vowing "nevermore," then toasts them dry in the oven in the middle of the night. I am a scavenger in ashtrays, a comber of the trash. I have been known to palm a cigarette from a pack left unattended on the bar. I have huffed smoke out bathroom windows. I have bummed hundreds of cigarettes from strangers. If there is a smoking-related degradation I have not experienced, please tell me what it is. I have studied myself-the-addict closely enough to know a few things the literature of quitting omits to mention.

For instance, smoking is not an oral but an emotional and meta-bolic fixation. Dis-stress makes me reach for the nearest nicotine de-livery system, sure, but so does eu-stress, the good stuff—inspiration, excitement, thoughts I've never thought before. These, too, I seek by habit to suppress. I use cigarettes to write a period to a meal, as an appetite curb. I use cigarettes and the exile of the contemporary smoker to build little oases of solitude into my life. Smoking is so closely entwined with writing that they are quite literally symbiotic activities for me.

I use cigarettes to micromanage my central nervous system and my moods. Nicotine speeds up the digestion and acts as a kind of laxative; in its absence, all the thousands of villi in the intestines slow from allegro to andante. Not only do you eat more, you absorb more of what you eat. Thus stomach cramps, flatulence, constipation, and weight gain are common side effects of quitting. There is a period during any attempt to quit when the compromised blood vessels in the extremities begin to open up again that feels like hundreds of tiny worms on speed are wriggling inside your fingers and toes. When the doctor or the American Lung Association tells you the physical symptoms of withdrawal pass within five to ten days, what they mean is, that's how long it takes the worms to die.

On this day, August 14, 1997, I have never once lasted through the death of the last worm.

On this day, I have come to the river to ask Ochun for her help. Having found my true love at last, I am not eager to die. I do not want to be a wrinkled old woman before my time. It is my fondest wish to celebrate my fiftieth birthday as a nonsmoker.

On this day, I am not entirely sure I believe it is possible to beat my addiction.

I wade out into the middle of the river nonetheless and make myself sit down in the deepest part of the riverbed, in water so icy when it touches my stomach and my sex, my breasts and thighs, that for the better part of a minute, I can't breathe. Heat flows out of me. My flesh grows cool and slippery as a trout's. When I lean back into the current, the river reaches up to play with my hair. Like weeds, strands fan across my shoulders in slow, sensuous motion. Then I lean back all the way, submerging my head. The coldness is headache and it is clarity. The river is loud in my ears. My prayer is bubbles, rising to the surface.

Please. Please wash me clean.

Five days later, we sit outside in the gathering dusk—me, Schuyler, and Schuyler's old friend Adam, a gifted raconteur, a hearty drinker, a chain-smoker. Normally, I would try to rev myself up to Adam's speed, to make the conversation a dance, a high-wire act, an event, but tonight I'm feeling disabled. It is five days since I smoked a cigarette, and everything about me is rather slow. I am used to words rushing like river currents through my brain, splashing up in jets of spray when they hit on new ideas, but tonight my brain is parched. Where have the words gone? The inside of my head is like a summer morning without birdsong. The silence feels unnatural. Besides, I want Schuyler's friend Adam to think that he's married a smart, funny woman. You know, cool.

Tonight I am anything but cool. If this is life without nicotine, I'm not sure it is worth living.

A few glasses of wine do much to melt my resolve. Schuyler goes in the house to find a book. Adam goes in the house to pee. He leaves his Marlboros on the table. Soon that pack of cigarettes is the only thing I can see, the only thing I can think about. Even with the first of the worms beginning to die, it is bigger, *much* bigger, than my will.

Before I really even know what I'm doing, I've slipped one perfect virgin cigarette out of Adam's red-and-white pack, I've tucked it up the sleeve of my tee-shirt, where it won't bend or break, I've hidden Adam's Bic lighter inside the pocket of my jeans, and I'm headed out of the courtyard for the backyard. I make it without being seen. I hide behind the garage, I light the cigarette, my hands are shaking.

How many times have I experienced this reward of almost quitting—the first hit of nicotine in the system, as dramatic as any high I've ever known, a superb disorientation. Here it comes. I make ready to take a drag from the stolen Marlboro, the biggest and most important cigarette in the universe. Oh, yeah.

As soon as the cigarette touches my lips, it is knocked from my hand and I am knocked from my feet, landing hard and unceremoniously on my ass on the ground. When I try to move, I find that I am paralyzed. From here, I can see the red eye of the cigarette, which has sailed far beyond my reach. It flickers and goes dark.

I'm stunned, of course, though I am perfectly okay. I've not had a heart attack or a stroke. I have simply experienced an answer to my prayers.

Once I realize this, I regain the power to move. I crawl over close enough to the garage to lean my back against it and laugh until my stomach hurts. I have not attempted to smoke another cigarette since.

Ochun has saved me from myself.

26

wedding clothes

It's April, and a sheet of pale sun folds at the window sill, bends again where wall meets floor, then comes to rest in a crisp pentagon mostly on the rug, all but unnoticed as my mother and I stand before her open closet, surveying the contents.

"I like this," my mother says, a little tentatively, stroking a mottled blue-and-white silk sleeve.

The fabric's nice, but the outfit dates back a good ten years, when my mother was considerably stouter than she is now. "Don't think it fits you anymore. How about this?"

"The skirt's too short."

"I'd be happy to take you shopping. It would be fun."

"No it wouldn't," my mother says. "Besides, I have plenty of clothes."

"This then." I pull out a rose silk skirt, mid-calf length, a rose/gold/green silk vest, and the silky white blouse that goes with them.

My mother touches the scalloped collar of the blouse. "Pretty," she says. "Where did it come from?"

"I bought it for you, last fall."

"I don't think I've ever seen it before."

"Sure you have. You wore it on Valentine's Day. You wore it . . ."

"I've always liked that color. They used to call it 'ashes of roses.'"

"It looks very pretty on you. Shall it be this, then?"

"Isn't the skirt awfully long?"

"Elegant. Besides, it's a wedding."

"Who's getting married?"

"I am, Mom. I'm marrying Schuyler, next Saturday."

"I'm surprised at you, getting married again. I didn't think you would."

"Hope springs eternal, Mom. Do you want to try it on?"

"Well, all right."

We shuck my mother out of her favorite black knit skirt, her black jacket and rust-colored blouse. Most of the ladies at the Grosvenor House affect an urban casual style, but left to her own devices, my mother reaches for something that looks like a business suit, which may be one reason among many that she is left to her own devices. She buttons the white blouse from the bottom, I from the top. We meet in the middle. Put on the vest. My mother studies her image in the mirror. "Ooooh." She half-turns left, then right, mostly to make that sibilant skirt whisper around her legs.

"What jewelry?" My mother's jewel box looks like a small armoire. The doors open to reveal three drawers. When the lowest is pulled out, a music box plays "Around the World in Eighty Days." It was her Christmas gift from me, my first year out of college and working in New York. We start with the chest and work deeper into her real bureau, browsing through the contents of little boxes hidden among the scarves and underwear. Heirlooms mostly. My mother's father often gave my grandmother expensive jewelry—engraved, custom-made, and much more ostentatious than she was comfortable wearing. This ring, for example—five big perfectly matched diamonds, representing their five sons, interspersed with three ruby daughters—has probably never seen the light of day. Finally we find a matching pendant and bracelet, gold and black onyx with clear crystal, an elegant Art Deco design. According to the family story, my father spent a whole summer hauling wheat in eastern Washington, then spent most of his earnings on this gift for his girl. More than sixty years later it still delights her eye. I fasten the pendant around her neck. For a moment, we admire the effect.

It's a moment outside of time. In it, my mother is beautiful, now as then and for all ages. The creases, sags, bumps, and bags of eighty-four years are there, all right, the stray coarse hairs sprouting from lip and chin, but good genes will out. The fundamental pleasingness, that flowerlike quality, still reside in her visage, a riddle and a ghost. I find a mostly used-up lipstick in her purse and give it to her to put on. She is pleased as a child by the difference a little color makes. Smiles back at the pretty white-haired girl in the mirror.

"This is it, then. Okay, Mom?"

"This is what?"

"Your wedding outfit. Mother of the bride."

"Am I going with you?"

"Orky and Ervin are picking you up. You'll get dressed with me and Alexandra at my house. It'll be fun, all three of us girls. Then we'll all go to the Grange together."

"The Grange?"

"Uh-huh. It's a potluck wedding, remember?"

"I won't know anybody," my mother says.

"Family. Old friends. You'll know a lot of people. If you're not having a good time, Orky or Alexandra can take you over to my house. You can take a nap."

Now my mother runs a hand back through her hair, silver-gray and flat at the end of a permanent cycle. "What am I going to do with this? I can't go anywhere looking like this."

"You have a hair appointment on Friday. New perm. You can have your nails done, too."

"Where?"

"Right here in the building. In the shop downstairs."

"But I don't like the shop downstairs."

"They have a new girl, Mom. I went and met her myself, to make sure you'd like her."

"Do you think you're going to be happy?" my mother says.

"Yes, I do."

"That's good." My mother nods, apparently satisfied. "Now, how am I getting to the wedding?"

And so, I explain again. I make a list of the key points, what time they're supposed to happen. Orky's phone number. Mine. A note to myself to call her. A note to the beauty parlor, saying come get her if you need to. Little safety nets strung across the days. Lessons in patience. It's the small stuff my mother forgets. After eighty-four years, I tell myself, she has a right.

It's a strange time, this. For nine months I have been courting, falling in love. While I've spent as much time with my mother as ever, my heart's been looking elsewhere. Overlooking what grows more and more evident. Three children between me and my intended shape, nip, truncate the tree of love. My mother more and more a fourth. I pray for the sweetness to last its due season. Schuyler is brave, to love a woman with so many obligations. For the moment, I take my mother at her word. She does not ask for changes in her living arrangements, will not assent to my suggestions. Prefers these small serial alterations. Her freezer compartment is full of Lean Cuisine.

I tape the list of reminders to the bathroom mirror. Pick up my keys. Put on my sweater. I have my mother's outfit on a hanger, her jewelry in a little box in my purse.

"Where are you going with that? If *you* wear that, what am *I* going to wear?"

"You're going to wear it, Mom. I'm just taking it home now, so you can get dressed with me on Saturday. Okay?"

"I don't have a wedding present for you."

"Coming to my wedding is your present." I kiss my mother's cheek. As usual, she startles slightly, then wipes the kiss away with the back of her hand. "Well, okay," she says.

"Saturday, then. I love you, Mom."

"Uh-huh," she says.

I make for the elevator, but don't step on until I hear the click shut of her door.

27

why I must decline (Anne's turn)

I know. I have always liked knowing. I won an essay
contest once. Now I am not sure what I know
or when I know it. I. Know.
I know they talk about me.
They whisper. Laugh. I don't know why. I do know
what it is like to not know
To be THERE, suddenly, and have no idea where THERE is
either as an address in space or in time.
To be THERE is to be imprisoned in a single moment
unplugged from the previous moment unable to anticipate
the one that's coming.
It's quiet I'll grant you that
and the trick I'm learning
(slowly painfully) is HERE as an antidote to THERE.
If I am always HERE
then I am in no danger of being
THERE getting stuck THERE
which is a place/time with a physical aspect
you might call panic and
wouldn't be misspeaking.
It is a heart beating at least doubletime.
It is dizzy.
Light head and heart crazy.
I am afraid of leaving
this set of rooms my body has memorized.

Someone is hiding my possessions.
Sometimes I am afraid it is me
hiding my possessions.
I hate not knowing.
I hate not knowing.
Like being onstage
only the first ten rows of the house seats
don't exist. It's not like they're empty
more like they've been removed from the theatre
or else the fog machine has gone berserk
obscuring the better part of the audience.
All strangers are ugly and most are cruel.
They move their mouths at me
grotesque really
the way they chew on words with their mouths open
quite rude I wish they would just
spit it out. I wish they would try
to make a little bit more sense.
Who swallowed the script?
She has gotten married so many times
I am tired of pretending to be happy about it.
I am tired of hoping it is not yet another mistake.
All marriage is mistake.
We just handle disappointment differently
she and I. God knows
I have tried. Sweet jesus I need to pee.
Maybe already have. The world less distinguishable
from nightmare every day. I am tired of smiling.
Most of the time I am afraid.
Some of the time I am afraid of myself.
Most of the time time is meaningless as skteheorihjekekdjd.
Can't tell if it's coming or going. She can

get married without me this time.
I would rather be a disappointment than a disgrace.
Time to pee goddamn pantyhose she will have to
understand. She will have to forgive me for knowing my limits.
For hiding my limits from her.

saying yes

What my mother told me on the phone was that she wasn't coming to my wedding because she wouldn't enjoy herself. I begged and cajoled and then, in the face of her unyielding, gave up.

"Mom, there's a pay phone in the basement of the Grange. I'll call you just before I get married. Then it will be almost like you're there. Okay?"

"Okay," she said.

"Be by the phone. Five o'clock. Okay?"

"Okay," she said.

When everything was ready that afternoon, the guests assembled, our friend-ministers, his and hers, waiting to perform the ceremony, Orpheus's lament for Eurydice playing over the speakers, I dropped thirty-five cents into the gummy old-fashioned pay phone in the basement of the Bainbridge Island Grange and dialed my mother's number. She answered promptly. I asked her for her blessing.

"For what it's worth," my mother said. Her voice was kind.

I thanked my mother.

Schuyler wiped my tears away. We went upstairs and got married.

29

money & fear

In her last season of competence, my lawyer-mother had her lawyer draw up three powerful documents—a general durable power of attorney; a clean, simple will that circumvented the need for probate; and a living will that authorized pulling the plug on life support in the case of prolonged and irreversible unconsciousness. Creating these instruments was canny, decisive, responsible, and, if her subsequent behavior is any indication, very hard for her. Having commissioned, received, and reviewed these documents, she waited another four months before signing her name on the dotted line. The corrected dates of execution bear witness to her reluctance to give up control of her affairs.

The most instruction my mother gave me regarding the stewardship of her personal business was to show me where to find the papers. There was no catalogue of assets, no helpful investment advice, no list of personal priorities or wishlist for the end of life. She did not describe to me at what point it would be timely to invoke my power of attorney. Whether this was a copout, an expression of trust, or a test of my integrity, I'll never know for sure. I do know I found myself feeling the way I used to on the schoolground, playing jump rope, in that long moment one watches the turners turning, the rope going round and round, trying to pick just the right moment to run in and start jumping. The longer one hesitates, the less likely it becomes the entry will be clean. Performing itself is not nearly so stressful as commencing to perform. Would the revolution be bloodless, or should I expect my mother to resist?

For a season or two, I resorted to halfway measures—a monthly bill-paying night; collecting all the paperwork and going together to the accountant at taxtime; adding my name to her bank accounts in advance of extremity. Each of these innovations was met with less protest than I expected. Still, my reluctance to take charge of my mother's finances was strange, almost pathological, especially since I was her only child and sole heir. The intensity of my feelings led me to take a hard look at my beliefs about money, to look below the surface, to the place where subtext and story come together. In those murky waters, I found these hidden premises: Money is imbued with emotional and ethical capital. It is not just currency, not just opportunity or freedom from the tyranny of a boss besides oneself, it is not just buying power or peace of mind, but a standing invitation to betrayal.

the tunnel-builder's death

By 1926, Olaf Olson, builder of tunnels through mountains, was rich, respected, and stone-blind. According to hearsay—what my Aunt Olga, who acted as his secretary, told her daughter Orky—he was so mentally acute and adept at his trade that he could visualize plans and spec construction materials, costs, and schedules pretty much off the top of his head, his sightlessness no handicap in this phase of the work. His five sons all worked with and for him, putting muscle behind the old man's mind. In the last weeks of his life, Olaf was bidding on what would have been the biggest job of his career. Competition was heavy, but according to the Canadian Pacific Railroad magazine, his was the favored firm.

And so, it is the Fourth of July, and my grandfather is in Vancouver, British Columbia, staying in the quietly grand Hotel Vancouver, which is his home away from home. My grandfather falls from the open window of his third-floor hotel room and lands, dead, on the sidewalk below. Newspaper accounts call the death an accident, attributable to his impaired sight. Years later, my mother tells me it was most likely murder.

Grandpa Olson's second-in-command was not one of his boys, but a foreman who kept the books and ran the camps. Family legend has it he was "no good." He deliberately sowed dissent among the five sons and spoke ill of them to their father in order to shore up his own position. Somehow, irregularities were detected in the books. On that July Fourth, the story goes, my grandfather confronted his foreman with the evidence of embezzlement. The foreman pushed Olaf out of the window and disappeared. British Columbia law enforcement didn't pursue him or the case because the victim was a foreign national. For them to have acted, my grandmother would have had to "press charges" through "diplomatic channels." Mathilde declined, saying, "It won't bring Olaf back."

That's the story I grew up believing.

In my mother's last years, I also came to believe that hers was a family that agreed upon certain stories and then closed ranks around them. I know that I will never know what really happened—what really happened in those construction camps or inside that big white "mansion" with its whitewashed concrete walls, its gabled green roof, its deep shaded porches, its balconies, its maze of bedrooms. I will never know what happened in that third-floor hotel room on the Fourth of July, how Olaf fell to his death. I do know that my mother was terrified of dying, because of a person or persons who had died before her, who in her last years taunted and threatened her from some shadowy other place that she saw clearly and we could not.

Money corrupts. That is the moral of this story. It has been handed down to me, even if all the facts have not.

30

it hits the fan

Because I was a contract employee, my office had no window. Instead of using the fluorescent overhead, I had a halogen lamp in one corner that cast a gentle light around the little room, a trick of décor much favored among employees of the Microsoft Network in its first bold, misguided incarnation. I was the editorial director of an interactive music show so cutting-edge that the technology needed for it to perform well wouldn't be widely available for another three or four years, but we had a splendid team of strange and talented people, a passion to pioneer, and the chance to spend large amounts of Bill Gates's money in pursuit of our collective dream. It was my job to interview our featured musicians and, in concert with a couple of designers, developers, and audio engineers, invent some new, interactive ways to present the results.

Preparing for the interviews, I listened with intense concentration to my subjects' music, trying to hold my mind and my heart open to its effects. And I read every review and interview I could lay my hands on, hundreds of pages, sometimes, so that I knew what stories the artists were used to telling about themselves. Once I understood the personal mythology, I looked for discrepancies, for places of tension, for evidence of courage or longing, for the things the music told about the life and psyche, and my interviews started there, slightly beyond where other interviews left off. My other, equally important trick was *listening*, something interviewers all too seldom do, so that my "next" question would come not from a script but from genuine curiosity about what had just been said. It was a fiction writer's take on the task, a way of deconstructing character, reversing the process of building human beings from scratch. It seemed to work. People told me extraordinary things. Many of them said they saw themselves and their lives in new ways because of our conversations. For that moment in time, it was the very best job I can even imagine having had.

I was doing it, then, editing transcript of my three-plus-hour interview with B. B. King. I had a huge amount of source material and a date at a recording studio to pull and edit audio clips the next morning. It was already clear I'd be working late that night when the phone rang. It was the Grosvenor House.

"When the maid let herself in to change the linens, she found your mother on the floor, covered with . . . well, you know, with feces," the woman said. She was the assistant manager, I think.

"What happened? Is she all right?"

"She seems to be all right. Not too clear about what happened, or when."

"But it wasn't a heart attack or a stroke?"

"Just really bad diarrhea, I think. The bedroom and bathroom are quite a mess."

I'm getting the picture, and it's not appealing. The tone of the woman's voice suggests there's something she's not saying. "Um, can the housekeeping staff help out with that?" I ask her.

"Not their job," the assistant manager informs me. "They already have their rounds, you know—so many units every day."

She's saying, *You. You come.* I say, "Know of anyone who'd like to make a little extra on their day off?"

"Afraid not," she says. "Besides, your mother needs cleaning up, too."

"Ah." I'm remembering the first *Star Wars* movie, the scene where all the good guys are in the giant trash compactor with the walls closing in. She's telling me I'm supposed to leave work and clean up shit. I'm thinking, *But I wanna edit B. B. King*. I'm thinking, *It would be hard enough to tell my boss I have to leave because I have a sick kid, let alone an elderly mother who just pooped her room*. My boss is a dozen years younger than I am. Her mother still has a day job. "Ah." I'm stalling. Then, inspiration. When the assistant manager asks what I intend to do, I have a plan. "Listen, I'm going to call the nursing service we used when my father was sick. I'll get a nurse over there right away. If my mother needs to see a doctor, they can go in a taxi. And I'll come straight there after work."

This seems to satisfy the assistant manager, who is, at this moment, an all-purpose stand-in for the invisible censor, that force of the universe that weighs my filial actions and omissions on finely calibrated scales. The avatar of the censor that lives inside me is less forgiving, insisting that anything less than a personal appearance, armed with mop and Lysol, is shirking my sacred duty. During my father's final illness, I was writing a novel in my bedroom office, just twenty minutes away. Any call for aid was answered immediately. I had no excuses and no boundaries then. My life was laid siege by my parents' misfortunes, to the detriment of my children and my work. In the middle of many nights, I have promised myself I would find a new way to be when it came my mother's turn, a way to be helpful without being subsumed. In the brown light of my contingent staffer's office, I take a deep breath. The overture is playing; somehow I recognize that tune. The show's about to begin. I find myself praying for the ability to feel many feelings at the same time, joy as well as sorrow, excitement as well as fear. As long as I can still be me, too, perhaps being mother's little helper won't be so bad.

After I've found and dispatched a nurse, I call my mother. Her voice is how I hate hearing it, old and flat, as if it is impossible even to imagine thirty seconds of soul-ease or pure happiness occurring at some unspecified future time. Life is unsatisfactory. Death is unavoidable. The whole scenario is quite unacceptable. My mother sounds implacably weary. It is a tic of my character that I meet her gloom by chirping.

"The nurse sounds really nice," I burble into the phone. "She'll be able to take your vital signs and assess your condition. She'll help clean up and make you something to eat that won't upset your stomach."

"All I need is some stranger bustling around here," my mother says.

"It's *exactly* what you need right now," I tell her.

"Listen, Joyce, I don't think this is a good idea." My mother speaks in the tone that's meant to shut me down, to deflect my initiatives in favor of her entropy, but something has shifted between us, perhaps shifts in this instant. I can no longer take the easy road. Time to stand up to her, for her own good.

"She's on her way, Mom. You'll really like her. And I'll come by and see you on my way home from work."

"I'll like her like the Jews liked Hitler," my mother says. "This is a crock of milk."

"Trust me, Mom," I say. She is quiet for so long that I begin to suspect she's hung up. "Are you there? Mom, are you still there?" Finally, after numerous inquiries, a few weary syllables trudge through our silence. An ironic huff, a grunt of resignation. "I'll see you later, Mom," I say. "I've got a lot of work to finish up here."

"I don't like it," my mother says. Now she really does hang up.

By the time I get to my mother's apartment, around seven, she likes it very much indeed. Nurse Nora is portly and good-humored, a sixtyish woman with just the hint of an English accent she's all but outlived. My mother is clean, cozy, beaming, her cheeks pink from an afternoon's companionship.

"Your mother is a charming woman," Nurse Nora says. "We've had a lovely time."

It's clear they have. There is a girl who lives inside my mother, impish and flirtatious. She loves to be the center of attention. She is so entertaining she *deserves* to be the center of attention. This is not the middle-aged monopolizer of conversations, it is not the elderly recluse, but a sweet and playful child. My seeing much of her is still a couple of years off; this night, she peers out of my mother's aged face, confused by my presence, not knowing whether to emerge or stay hidden. I am relieved to find she has banished the aged, hopeless crone I talked to earlier, glad some sweetness has returned to my mother's cup. I grin at her. She makes a funny face at me, wrinkling her nose and scrunching up her eyes.

Nurse Nora has fed my mother. She has collected all her medications into one place and made a flowchart of what should be taken when. She has called my mother's doctor to revise one of her prescriptions; it's so strong that if my mother accidentally took an extra pill, she'd do herself serious harm. She has taken notes on my mother's condition, her vital signs, and her own conversation with the doctor. In her opinion, my mother may have had a tiny stroke, or she may simply have become severely dehydrated as a result of the diarrhea and fainted. My mother obviously feels safe. Not since Ethel died have I seen her so relaxed in the company of another woman. I feel the tension that's been my companion all day lift a bit.

Nurse Nora asks to speak to me privately. We leave my mother in front of the television set and head to the kitchen for our chat.

"Mum's not remembering properly," Nurse Nora tells me. "She oughtn't to be left alone. Not until you disconnect that stove, anyway. I'm afraid she'll leave it burning and start a fire."

With her help, I waltz the range far enough from the wall that I can reach behind with a barbecue fork and pull the plug. My mother calls to us from the living room to come and see the elephants. The elephants are on TV. I hang around for maybe an hour more before I head for the ferry to complete my journey home, and it's like visiting a couple that's settled in and comfortable together. My mother loves to be pampered, and Nurse Nora is a pro. She seems to enjoy the job. Definitely, I am odd woman out.

I have put my mother on the waiting list for Assisted Living. Until a unit becomes available, the rent-a-nurse option will have to suffice. Twelve hours a day, well timed, should keep my mother out of harm's way. In fact, she likes this solution so much, that she gets angry at me for suggesting it's time to move. This is how she wants to live, with a personal servant who doubles as captive audience. The only problem is, apart from being in poor shape, apart from her memory deficit, my mother is healthy as a horse. She may well live another ten years, another fifteen. Private nursing costs an extra three hundred dollars a day. Even if it is her money, the numbers don't add up.

As I kiss my mother goodnight—yes, she wipes it away—as I thank Nurse Nora and make my way to the ferry dock through rain-slick streets, some quiet small part of me remembers the pleasure of interviewing B. B. King.

Anxiety, it occurs to me, is often more a creature of our ego than a virtue of our love.

31

guerrilla tactics

Grosvenor House management assures me that former "Apartments Plus" residents who've moved into Assisted Living "do so much better" it's practically "miraculous." This is, of course, exactly what I want to hear, because, truth told, my mother isn't doing very well at all. Sometime between Mother's Day on the third Sunday in May and the brunch we hold to celebrate my daughter's high school graduation on the second Sunday in June, her weight declines and her confusion mounts noticeably, in inverse proportion, even though an LPN comes in one shift a day, gets her dressed and gives her her medications, makes sure she eats two reasonably respectable meals. If a stroke's the culprit, it's left no physical sign, and she has no memory of an unusual event, but the change is almost shocking.

On Mother's Day, when I came into the city to pick her up and take her back to my house on Bainbridge Island, she knew I was coming and was mostly dressed when I arrived. Her physical strength and muscle tone were compromised enough by chronic inactivity that our progress up the ferry terminal ramps was slow, but with my help and her cane's, she made it under her own steam. Three weeks later, my knock echoes through the quiet hallways, louder and louder as it meets with no response. I go down to the lobby and call her number. No answer. Finally, since I've left my keys at home, I get the security guard to let me in. Apprehension settles on my shoulders like a cold and prickly shawl.

Anne lies on her back in the brass bed she was born in, her features scrunched together as if she's trying hard to solve a baffling riddle. The noise of my entry, my calls of "Mom? Mom!" do nothing to animate her stillness. I'm struck with a profound sense of her absence. My heart slams in my chest as I kneel beside her bed and take her hand. Her hand is cool but feels supple, like living flesh. I rub it between my own. "Mom! Mom, wake up." I shake her shoulders. "Mom."

At last she comes back from wherever she's been, a long journey, marked by coughs and wheezes and a startle as her eyes open and she sees me there, so close by—Who? Huh? Slowly, consciousness comes and my mother knows who I am, if not where I came from or why I am here.

Having come so far, I'm afraid of resistance, of the kind she mustered on my wedding day, but find now that as long as I provide a kind of relentless momentum, she will allow herself to be borne along. This willingness is new. It holds through a cup of coffee, a spit bath, dressing, grooming, a prolonged search for her purse which, since the nurses have been coming, she's taken to hiding. She looks quite pretty in her Mother's Day blue silk jacket and seems quite present by the time we make our way downstairs.

Downstairs, we find that the taxi I asked to wait has given up on us. It takes twenty minutes or so for another to come fetch us. At Colman Dock, the ramps my mother was able to negotiate three weeks before are totally beyond her today. A kind-looking stranger agrees to stay with my mom while I head off to find a wheelchair in the terminal. On the ferry crossing, my mother sits by the window and stares out at the ruffled gray water in deep and silent contemplation, as if she's replenishing her energy, hoarding her language for the social trial ahead. After a few attempts at conversation, I assent to her silence and let myself, too, sink below the surface of word and detail to a gray, still place.

When we arrive at my house, almost three hours later than expected, the party is in full progress. My daughter rushes to hug her grandma. Many of our guests are family; they crowd around to greet my mother, and she warms to their attention. While she visits, I fetch her a plate of food. My husband has carried on without me, and even though it's mostly been consumed by the time we get there, it looks as if the buffet brunch was a great success. No one seems to mind that I'm still in my blue jeans and sneakers, with no makeup on. Schuyler gives me a hug and a cup of coffee. The day's greatest reward is finding that my mother has absolutely no recollection of my former husband, the father of my children, who is attending the festivities with his new wife. My mother shakes his hand and responds to his double-edged small talk with a look of quizzical civility.

Near the end of the afternoon, Schuyler takes a picture—my son, my mother, my daughter, me—our arms around each other, from the chest up. In the picture, you can see the play of genes across our four sets of features, see the similarities in the shape of chins, the arch of eyebrows, even, in the case of me and my children, in the gaze we turn upon the world. What will the next adventure be? My mother's stare is more direct, almost accusatory, as if she is wise to your bullshit, to all your self-deceptions, and finds them tiresome, as if she won't waste her precious energy being disappointed or surprised. Her gaze is penetrating and shrewd, suspicious, the look of a highly intelligent small mammal. When I first see the photograph, the look seems new, another of the day's revelations. A couple of years later, though, grazing through fields of old family pictures with my mother, I find that it is the same look she wore as a girl of six or seven. In her school pictures, in family snapshots, Anne is an unsmiling, hard-eyed, skeptical child, as deep and inward as a black hole. This disaffection persists for half a dozen years or so, until a radiant young adolescent suddenly appears.

The graduation party is, by all reports, a fine affair. By the time I've returned my mother to the Grosvenor House, tucked her in bed, and come back to the island, it's well after ten o'clock at night. Next day's commute to work starts with the six-twenty boat. I am deeply aware that, were I still a single mother, this day would have gotten away from me entirely. As it is, I've had my first chastening lesson in dealing with dementia—time is not of the essence. It may not even be real. Schedules are the vain illusion of those who believe themselves to be in control, yet another concept that falls before the alchemical changes of a deteriorating brain.

By now it is clear to all of us that my mother can no longer live alone.

Somebody died, leaving a spacious studio unit vacant in Assisted Living. Management steam-cleaned the carpet and the drapes. I signed the check and the stack of waivers, took my mother to the Polyclinic for the required physical, even though she'd had one only a few weeks before, and hatched a plan. My mother would not hear of moving. The choices involved—what to take, what to discard, what to pass on, what to store—far exceeded her tolerance for stress. Under the guise of a series of routine social visits, I scoped out her furniture and other effects, trying to imagine what would fit in the studio, where, and to intuit which of her possessions were the most essential to a sense of continuity, of security, and grace. I was hoping for a kind of decorator impressionism, that the right objects properly deployed would evoke their absent comrades and create the illusion that nothing was amiss. Some of my choices were based on Anne's declarations of affection or admiration for this thing or that; the rest reflected my own sense of what was necessary to my mother's world. Most things I selected as keepers were part of the décor of my childhood home. Many came from the Maple Valley mansion where she grew up.

The move was a guerrilla action. My children, my cousin, and her husband took my mother out to the city's most leisurely brunch, while Schuyler and I and one of Alexandra's brawny teenaged suitors undertook to move her things. We worked swiftly, mostly in silence. After two hours, everything was in place. We paid the boyfriend, made the bed, set out the towels and toilet articles, raced to the nearby supermarket for fresh flowers and a bottle of champagne, and then were done. Dusty, sweaty, we perched on the concrete wall in front of the building and chain-smoked cigarettes while we waited for my mother to return.

At last the car pulled up. My son handed my mother out, and we all waited for Alex to park before we went inside. We formed a chevron around my mother, spirited her through the lobby and into the elevator. Once there, we pressed two, instead of thirteen.

"That's not my floor," she said.

"We just have to make a little stop on the way," I said.

On two, we spilled out of the elevator, still in formation, and walked my mother into Assisted Living the long and formal way, so that it looked its best.

"Where are we going?" she asked.

We traded looks. "You'll see, Grandma," my son said, taking her arm.

When we reached her new studio, I opened the door and stood back to let the others flow inside. The space looked hospitable, handsome, familiar. The kids made faces, communicating both approval and apprehension. My mother made a noise, something between a grunt and a whistle, and I heard something else, too, a refusal on its way to utterance, but it never quite arrived. Instead, she slowly turned, a full three hundred and sixty degrees, taking in all aspects of her new apartment, then sighed. "I guess I live here now," she said.

nolo contendere (Anne's turn)

My mother's statue of napoleon
My mother's statue of napoleon

My mother's statue of napoleon
Tarnished brass
The bed where I was born
The secretary with its hidden drawers
With secrets in the hidden drawers
What is missing shouts
Remember me
But
I do not remember
They watch me
Expectantly and I choose
To not remember
In this one case
Forgetfulness becomes
a virtue
how can I miss
what I cannot recall
something has been amputated
in this one case
forgetfulness becomes
an anaesthetic
equal parts
gratitude and rage
my life henceforth becomes
a phantom limb
and they are right
it is true
never would I authorize
diminishment
never would instigate
this little death
but yet I stipulate

the deed is done
pass me the glass
and I will toast
the end of all things
known

32

ancestors

Here in the New World, the idea of ancestor is hard.

Those who came in chains were victims of an uprooting so thorough it left little or no trace of native soil. From a village-based life so ancient and vital that lineages could be traced backward even past the place where history melts into myth, African slaves were transported into a nightmare where one generation was torn from the arms of its progenitors, perhaps never to meet upon this earth again. Genealogies are impossible to maintain in such circumstances.

Except for the very few who sailed for these shores under commission from European monarchs, with license to subdue and exploit all they encountered, most everybody else headed *here* because things were rotten *there*. Our founding fathers and mothers were religious eccentrics, paupers, criminals—people, in short, to whom risking their lives and luck in an untamed wilderness, or an urban tenement, seemed like a good deal compared to whatever punishment, impoverishment, or persecution awaited them at home. Among immigrants, the severing of ancestral roots was voluntary, but in most cases no less complete.

In time out of memory, local religions may have tied living to ancestral generations in strong, benevolent connection, but in conquering the cultures of Europe, imperial Christianity ruthlessly sliced or burned these bonds. Those with a strong sense of family, of community, of a religious identity that derives from and supports both, are hard to tax, to manage, and subdue. The heresy of ancestor worship was severely punished and eventually obliterated. Later, science became the apologist for Christianity's spiritual genocide, dismissing the reverence for ancestors as primitive and superstitious. In Asia, in Africa, in regions of the world unconquered by the church militant, ancestor worship continues to this day to be practiced by highly sophisticated people, suggesting that it is neither. In any case, by the seventeenth century, when voluntary migration to the Americas began, Europeans were accustomed to seeing their progenitors not as ancestors but simply as the dead.

The first advice I received upon approaching Santeria was to create a boveda, an altar for my ancestors, and to begin a relationship with them. This is pretty much the first message any seeker receives, whether one is African, Hispanic, or some melting-pot stew cooked up of many ingredients—the road to orisha begins with eggun. No passage is possible until they are propitiated. This news is a sharp knife, one that cleaves the American psyche right up the middle.

On one level, connecting with one's ancestors makes perfect emotional sense. It ratifies whatever extraordinary experiences a sensitive person may have had of his or her dead. It satisfies a longing for continuity and creates a sense of community that transcends one's present address in space and time. It even hints at an ultimate connectedness among all of us who walk this earth on two legs. With one backhand blow, it strikes down existential angst: we are not alone. News of our self-creation has been greatly exaggerated.

The other, equally automatic response to the notion of relating to one's ancestors is a shriek of dismay. Are we not, above all things, *individuals?* Hey, I don't like my brother, much less my great-great-great-grandmother. Who knows what she was like, anyway? Me, revere those losers? You've got to be kidding. Whatever I am, whatever I accomplish is mine, all mine, attributable to me alone. I have no debt to the past and none to the future. That it's a short step from *Seize the day* to *Rape the planet* is subject for another discussion. The point is, the cult of the individual and the cult of eggun are, if not quite mutually exclusive, uneasy occupants of the same consciousness.

Give it a try. See what happens. I approached the making of my boveda with a doggedly open mind. Schuyler's table featured an attractive display of photos of dead people from both sides of his family, many of whom looked more or less like him. Even though visual aids are not strictly necessary, I liked the idea, if only as a way to make what seemed like a highly abstract idea more concrete. My excavations through drawers, boxes, and albums full of photos of both sides of my own family made me remember—in some cases, remember my personal experience of the living being, in others, the scraps of story attached to the names of people who died before or soon after I was born. Because for much of my life, I've been a storyteller by trade, because I'd sometimes drawn from family legends to create my fictions, I was aware of how strong is the impulse to mythologize, and how many the reasons are to do it—sometimes simply to make a better story, sometimes to fill in a hole left in the narrative, sometimes to satisfy a highly personal need for a hero or a villain at just that place on the family tree. I found myself getting hung up over the unreliability of family history, tangled in webs of affect and assessment that rose out of the stories I'd heard and the ones I'd unwittingly helped make up. There was much about my ancestors I didn't know, much I didn't understand, and some I didn't much like.

Schuyler assured me that once our dead are raised up to become our ancestors, they are no longer as they were in life—the flaws, the shortcomings, the disappointments, the prejudices, the pains are all left behind. The ancestors become spirit, pure and powerful. We take care of them and they return the favor. The living person abetted by ancestors is always stronger and more fortunate than the one who is estranged from them. In traditions where the connection is respectfully and enduringly maintained, you might say our ancestors are our luck, are our strength, our secret weapon. We surrender our sense of the incarnate individual. In return, we gain the assistance of the spiritual being.

Want to get into film school? Get that new job? Keep on that diet? Find love? Do you want the teachers you need to appear in your life? Me, I often pray at my table for the wisdom not to diminish reality by my definition of it. Keeping mind and spirit that far open is hard enough that it bears asking for assistance every day. The point is, from the grossly material to the magical and ephemeral, the well-tempered ancestor stands ready to help us out. Repeat after me: This is not superstition. It is psychologically profound, a powerful metaphor that in the practicing becomes a literal truth, as well.

It is also, as you may have observed, totally at odds with the "I am a piece of shit, not worthy to blah blah blah" school of prayer advanced by so many churches, particularly of the Judeo-Christian stripe. Addressing eggun, the idea is to pray to out loud, to identify oneself clearly, to state what one wants and needs, to ask for help in attaining it. In consideration for this assistance, to tend the shrine, to do honor, to give water, food, light, flowers, prayers, and yes, even company to one's ancestors. This theology assumes that you have an essential right to prosper, to be the best and most successful person you're inherently capable of becoming, to live in harmony with your fellows and with the earth itself. It assumes that you may indeed know what it is you want and need; should that not be the case, it provides you with ways of seeking counsel from both ancestor and orisha. Guilt is not required. Service is. So is ethical behavior.

If you've grown up otherwise, your soul fed on the notion of its own sinfulness, these are extraordinarily difficult premises to accept. Even if you see them as healthy and sane, even if you're willing to consider that one's relationship to the spiritual might be less feudal, more reciprocal, "thy will be done" has so thoroughly insinuated itself into our collective subconscious that disclaimers, hemmings and hawings, and apologies for asking come tumbling unbidden from our whispering lips. If you doubt me, just try to pray as if you have every right to the fulfillment of your heart's desires. Try to pray as if you really believe the entity to whom you're addressing your prayer is capable of granting your requests, of making you content and fulfilled, creative and prosperous beyond your wildest dreams.

Hard, isn't it?

Keep practicing.

"God" is bigger than you are, granted, more complex, more subtle and powerful and smarter than you can easily understand, but this doesn't mean he/she/they despise you or want to punish you or don't trust you to pray for worthy things. It simply means that it came to be in the best interests of religious institutions for you to believe that. It is neither empirically nor intuitively obvious that you are a wretched sinner deserving of damnation, only historically convenient. The fact is, people whose prayers are answered develop ethically. At this moment, I do not live in poverty. Love is abundant in my life. I have borne and raised my children. I am healthy and strong. I am excited about my work. When I pray, it's not for a newer car or a bigger house, but for the protection of my friends and family and our beautiful, abused planet. I pray to grow in my faith. I pray to fulfill my destiny. I am fifty-two years old, and my most frequent and fervent prayer is simply to be of use. Most of us, allowed to feel blessed and beloved, grow beyond selfishness in due season.

33

ducks and other birds

As I ran this morning, keeping to the shorn grass at the shoulder of the road, a hubbub rose up suddenly behind me—not the wing-flutter of a small bird moving from branch to branch, unseen in the tangled shrubs, but a big noise that wanted to be heard. As I listened, a female duck overtook me on the left, flying low in the channel of the drainage ditch beside the road. The duck exploded upward and swerved out over pavement, stunt-flying, then settled back into the low corridor, wings flapping at a furious pace. Her bravura reminded me of the virtuoso flying in the first *Star Wars* movie.

I looked down into the ditch just behind me. Sure enough, it was full of water, and there, mostly hidden in the tall green grass, I saw them: three fluffy ducklings out for what must have been one of the first swims of their lives. Mother was doing her job, duck as decoy, drawing my attention away from her offspring.

"Hey," I called after her, "come back. I won't hurt your babies," but the duck was not about to succumb to sweet talk. Only when I was gone, her babies would be safe. Her skepticism was unshakeable and enduring, hardwired into her very being. In that, the duck reminded me of my mother.

"Your mother, she don't want to do something, she puts up her middle fingers—like this—and shakes 'em at you." This is Lavinia, black, twentysomething, a nurse's aide. She's studying to be a beautician, which means she'd rather sit at the front desk and do her homework than mingle with the inmates. Still, she seems to get a kick out of my mother's spunk. Most of the old white ladies here are awfully quiet. Some folks have the summer-camp knack of latching on to a dinner partner—there's one constant couple, always eats together and yammers away top volume from iceberg lettuce to tapioca pudding—but there are a lot of solitaries, too, many too deaf or drugged to be good companions. One of the things my mother doesn't want to do is sit alone in that formal little dining room, looking lonely, listening to other people carry on. She likes it when I time my visits to coincide with dinnertime and sit with her while she eats, something that, given the exigencies of Microsoft and gridlock, it's often hard to do.

"We'll take her in her meals like she wants," Lavinia tells me, "but it costs you an extra five bucks a shot. That's fifteen a day. Adds up," she says.

I'll admit I'm spoiled. I have the kind of kids teachers love. They're bright, present, sometimes argumentative, but fundamentally respectful. Conferences always leave me feeling good about them, about myself. My mom, though, appears to be a hard case. Besides the meal thing, there's the matter of taking a shower. Won't do it, most times. Sittercise class? Hell no. Current events discussion group? Give me a break. Just getting her to leave her room for meals requires ingenuity. She does like to feed the fish in the big tank in the parlor—so much so, in fact, that she does it whether they need to eat or not. Fish lacking a mechanism to tell them when they've had enough, the result is a lot of dead fish.

"And you know, she still don't know which one is her room," Lavinia goes on. "We put those plastic flowers on the door so she could tell. And we put the sign on that other door, the one that leads out of here, that says, Don't go out this door."

"Very fairy tale," I say.

"Don't get me wrong, your mom's a real nice lady, but she can be a han'ful, you know what I mean?"

"I know what you mean," I say.

"I was thinkin' maybe you could have a little talk with her, you know?"

For some reason, this gets past all my defenses, and I find myself telling this young woman whom I scarcely know that my mother and I have had a "difficult" relationship for a long time, that my advice doesn't carry a lot of weight with my mother the retired lawyer, that I try to do the right thing anyhow. It's *hard.* Blithering on, I realize how much I want somebody to acknowledge how hard it is. I want somebody to tell me I'm a good girl. Probably, I want my mother to tell me I'm a good girl, but right now, anyone will do. I listen to myself, and I hear two things—a liberal dose of self-justification, and just how incredibly needy I sound.

Maybe middle-aged, middle-class children of the elderly infirm spin out a lot, because Lavinia takes my little soul-baring outburst with knowing calm. Instead of answering melodrama with melodrama, angst with angst, she pushes her pencil into the dense thicket of her hair and grins at me. "I hear you," Lavinia says. "My grandma is just plain ornery, too. She drives my mama crazy all the time."

My mother is in her pajamas, even though it's two o'clock in the afternoon.

"Been napping?" I ask her.

"No."

"You're not dressed."

"Why should I be?"

"Because they won't let you in the dining room unless you're dressed."

My mother gestures to the tray beside the door. "I ate something here."

"You're not supposed to have your meals brought to you unless you're sick."

"That's nonsense," my mother says.

"It's expensive, is what it is."

My mother shrugs.

"I hear you've been flipping off the nurses, Mom."

My mother's expression has been set hard, but now amusement dances across her face, settling in her small, bright eyes. "Who told you that?"

"Word gets around." My mother beams pridefully. Part of me finds this funny. Part is woefully exasperated. "You know they can throw you out of here if you give them too much of a bad time."

My mother shrugs.

"Don't you like your apartment?"

My mother looks around. "It's all right. But I don't like people coming in here and telling me what to do. It's time to get dressed, it's time to shower, it's time to eat, it's time to shit. It's a crock of milk, if you ask me."

"So you let your middle fingers do the talking." I'm thinking, I must confess, of the monthful of summer nights we've just spent emptying out my mother's apartment upstairs, trying to cope with her lifetime's accumulated *stuff*. Please, please don't make us have to move her again. Not for a while anyway.

"The thing is, they have a bunch of people to help out, so they need to keep a schedule."

"Well, *I* don't need to keep their schedule."

"Why not give it a try?"

"I know where that road leads," my mother says darkly.

We carry on like this a while longer, until a knock comes on the door.

"Now what is it?" my mother grumbles.

"Come on in," I say.

Lavinia enters, carrying a little white paper nut cup, a little waxy paper cup of water. "Miz Thompson? I got your pills."

"Oh really?" my mother says. "What pills are those, pray tell?" All of sudden she's slipped into a character, lovable mouthy child. Her body language has changed, spine straightened, and her voice is saucy.

Lavinia tips the little nut cup so that my mother can see the two capsules inside. "Dunno what they are," she says. "I do know you're supposed to take 'em."

"How do I know you're not trying to poison me?" my mother asks brightly.

"Jus' because," Lavinia says. "Come on, now. You take these or your daughter here will be thinkin' I don't know how to do my job."

"We wouldn't want that, now would we?" my mother says. She winks at Lavinia, then holds out her hand for the tablets, and Lavinia empties the contents of the little cup onto my mother's palm. My mother makes a point of studying the pills closely before she puts them in her mouth. Lavinia hands her the water cup and Anne swigs the capsules down. After she swallows, she says, "Do I get my merit badge now?"

"Sure," Lavinia says. "You get another one if you get yourself dressed by dinnertime."

"Maybe I will and maybe I won't," my mother says.

"You have a nice visit now," Lavinia says.

When she's gone, my mother lifts her palm to her mouth. When she brings it away, there's one slimy, half-melted capsule on her palm. She grins at me. "Sometimes I fool them," my mother says.

34

tripping

On the airplane, my mother sits between me and Schuyler. She refuses a magazine, the movie. Instead, the brown eyes dart, the white head swivels. She takes in everything—the pageant of fellow passengers, the antics of the attendants, the slightly grimy upholstery of the seat in front of her, even the screws that hold the plane together. Takeoff corrugates her forehead, and she clings tightly to my hand. When food comes, she falls upon the soggy hoagie, the limp lettuce and lardy cookie as if she has not eaten in weeks. Her expression seesaws between worry and awe. It is ten years, at least, since my mother has traveled by air.

In the face of the hardness of the last few months, we are running away from home, all four of us—Schuyler, Ian, my mother, and I. Change makes for challenge; the end of jobs and habits, the loss of independence, falls and failures have all beset us. My daughter has gone away to college and I miss her so much it feels like dying. Three of us know we are on our way to see her now. My mother knows she is having an adventure.

When we go to baggage claim in San Jose, my mother says, "I've been here before." As we drive south on Highway 17 in our rental car, she says, "Oh, yes, I recognize this road." The Santa Cruz campus, too, looks familiar. So does Alexandra's dorm. Thus, kindly, the unfamiliar domesticates itself for her. It's not until we're buzzed into the dormitory and knocking on Alex's door that strangeness overtakes her, and that doesn't last long. As soon as my daughter appears in the doorway, the world makes sense again, to my mother no less than to me.

Ian bursts through the door that connects our motel rooms. "Mom, you have to do something. Grandma's naked." He stays in our room with Schuyler while I go next door to investigate, to see what he's seen, a body with eighty-five years on the chassis, with cracks in the upholstery, nicks in the paint.

"Lose something, Mom?"

My mother blinks at me. "There was a young man in here just a little while ago. He startled me."

"That was Ian. Your grandson. You startled him, too."

"Where are we, do you know?"

"You're in room 216 of the Ramada Inn, Santa Cruz, California. You're doing just fine. What say you have a shower before we go out to see the butterflies?"

"Oh, I don't want to shower," my mother says. "I'm clean enough for butterflies."

She doesn't actually see them, those migratory monarchs, not in their full dense glory, anyway. The grotto of trees where they flock by the thousands lies at the bottom of a trail my mother finds too steep, so we take turns sitting with her at a shady picnic table in the park above, where only the occasional errant insect pierces the thin blue air of fall. Below, butterflies cover the branches of the trees like fur. The reverence they inspire arises from something more than sheer numbers. I think of my father. I wonder if each of these monarchs is fit to be a spirit's steed. At the top of the trail, my mother seems deeply content. She hums a little snatch of song. *Que sera, sera.*

My mother is game, then she's gone, swooning into a nap that spans afternoon and evening. One of us always stays with her. Sometime between five and seven, she wakes up. Her face crumples like old

Kleenex then, with the sheer force of concentration it takes to place herself in the reeling universe, and she is quiet, as if language were a creature of the morning, or she'd left it behind wherever she just was. Dressed in her housecoat, she finds us in the room next door and claims her share of the carry-out chicken, settles in to watch a movie with us.

My children sprawl with me on one king-size bed, but my mother prefers to sit in a chair. She gives the television her full attention, often talking back to the characters or commenting on the action as it unfolds. On the whole trip, the movie she likes best is *Men in Black*.

Schuyler appoints himself documentarian. In the motel room, on campus, in restaurants, wandering the streets of Monterey, inside the car, at the airport, he is always shooting, shooting. When the film is developed, there are hundreds of moments frozen from a fluid time, candid portraits, not just of people but of relationships between them, visual reminders of spoken words and warm skin, frowns and rows as well as laughter, with the strangers in the periphery acting as chorus and mirror, showing us ourselves through yet another set of eyes. There we are on the boardwalk, just seconds after the kids have dropped ice down my shirt; there's Ian on the roller-coaster and Schuyler in the organic garden at dawn; Anne walking up the sidewalk between me and Alex, swinging from both our arms.

Home, we sort through the photographs and mount a huge collage, three and a half feet by four. We give it to my mother. Schuyler intends it to take the place of memory, and so it does. It becomes the trip, a trip she takes until she dies.

35

Anne shares her dinner

It's Thanksgiving, the air basted with the mingled smells of roasting bird and baking pie, yellow flames dancing in the fireplace in apparent sync to the music. I'd be lying if I claimed to remember just what was playing, but Van Morrison's *Healing Game* is a good guess, or it might have been something by Jane Siberry, maybe *When I Was a Boy*. Let's say that's what it was. Siberry's "Love Is Everything" will be our soundtrack. My son Ian is mashing potatoes, my stepson Farrell setting the table. I'm making the gravy. Schuyler sharpens his carving knife, while Alex, my daughter, home from college, sits on the living room floor, making our little white dog do tricks, to the amusement of her grandmother, who is ensconced on the sofa with a cup of light coffee and maybe a morsel of smoked salmon on a cracker to tide her over till the meal is ready. My mother keeps her purse tucked up close beside her, even among family, and hides it from the helpers at the place where she now lives. She no longer uses money, although I make sure she always has a couple of bills and some change in her wallet, just in case. After two Assisted Living aides were caught stealing, I took her credit cards and cut them up, lest they fall into the hands of strangers and finance a vacation to Tahiti. Compact, lipstick, comb, keys, and pen—these, too, she has but never uses anymore. If I had to guess, I'd say that as everything else shifted around her, her purse, or the idea of purse, has come to represent identity. So long as purse is safe, so, too, is she.

That it is Thanksgiving is not a detail that sticks in my mother's mind. We all know and accept this by now, and so, in her way, does she, finding the information interesting each time it's relayed, in no way distressed by not knowing it already. She reaches out to pet the dog, Caspar, says something to him—"You're a cute little fellow, aren't you?"—and the dog leaps up into her lap. My mother startles a little, then pets the dog energetically. For a moment, they seem to invent a little game between them, grandma and dog, that amuses them both. It strikes me, at the stove, that they have in common living almost entirely in the present moment. For my mother, this is new.

In the old days, Anne was deliberate, analytical, long to weigh and slow to act. She could conjure up every possible pitfall of a course of action, with the result that while she rarely made mistakes, she often did nothing at all. Now, in the absence of a short-term memory, all she can do is act and be. The skeins of circumstantial evidence that account for where we are and what we're doing, right here, right now, are no longer available to her. Like Alice, Anne is always falling down the rabbit hole. The wonderful thing about it is, when she's with us, at least, she feels safe enough to surrender to that circumstance. This spontaneity is an unexpected gift of the disease. Caspar chases his tail. My mother crows with delight.

Our Thanksgiving feast is ready at last. Alex guides my mom to the bathroom, then to her place at table, while the rest of us dish up portions of our dinner on small white plates. My mother is intrigued.

"Surely you're not giving that to the dog," she says.

"No, Mom. It's for the ancestors."

"The ancestors?"

"Uh-huh. Like your mom and dad, and their parents, and Olga and Adeline and Emmett. All those people. They loved to eat. So we're sharing our dinner with them."

The idea is new, and she sits with it silently for a moment. Then she says, "Are they coming here?"

"Come with me and we'll give it to them." I help her up from the table and take her hand. Together, we carry the plate of food to the closet in our little dressing room, where Schuyler's boveda and mine stand side by side, aglow with candlelight, fragrant with white roses. My mother gives a little gasp, to see so many beloved, half-forgotten faces in one place. Her parents, her grandparents, her in-laws, all her brothers and sisters are there on the altar. Smiling, she leans close to see them better. My father, her husband, is there. For a moment, she is with them, wholly engaged. Then she steps back to stand beside me, and I speak to the ancestors, as I have learned to do. I tell them Anne is there with me, and we are sharing our Thanksgiving dinner with them. I tell them we are thankful for their presence in our lives, and that we have each other. I put the plate of food on the altar and wrap my arm around my mother's shoulders. Her body feels relaxed beside me. "So, what do you think?" I ask her.

I don't know what I expect her to say, what kind of derision or resistance she will cast up, and I brace myself, but a faint smile plays on my mother's lips, and without a trace of irony she says, "I think it's very nice."

36

the dark

Sometime between Thanksgiving and Christmas, my mother's lights went out for the first time. Her face changed, as if the pull of gravity on it had suddenly been many times enhanced, as if all the moisture had been sucked out of her skin, as if her eyes, were they windows, had been boarded shut. Most of us, moving through our lives, give off energy, shoot out little sparks of affect into the surrounding air, but in the dark times, my mother became profoundly, magnetically heavy, compacting all the light and love around her into a small dense core. To refuse became her one response to the living. I believe that to resist was her single mission with the dead.

This is both metaphor and a literal description of my mother's state.

A person with no short-term memory can't really tell you what's wrong, even when something clearly is. Through time and recurrence, I came to recognize the symptoms I've just described as the combined effects of depression, dehydration, malnutrition, the action of a virus or bacterium, and the response of the psyche to the approach of the passage that is death.

Take her to the doctor, Assisted Living said. Assorted doctors took their assorted tests and told me they found nothing wrong. My mother stared into the middle distance at apparitions that gave her no peace. She began to talk about the dead—her sisters and brothers, Ethel. Had I seen them lately? How were they doing? She felt bad, she said, being so long out of touch. The less she ate, the more delusional she got.

The aides in Assisted Living accepted my mother's refusals and fled her darkness. By Christmas Day, only I and her bladder could coax her out of bed. Our dinner was a cheerless picnic in her room. After she picked at her turkey for a little while, my mother crawled back into bed. She asked us to leave the bathroom light on when we left.

The doctors took more tests and told me they found nothing wrong.

It was New Year's Eve, when I took her to the bathroom, that I first saw the bedsore on her left flank. It was a deep, angry red, as big in circumference as a baking powder biscuit.

"What the hell is that?" I said.

"What?"

"That big red place on your bottom. How did it get there? Does it hurt?"

My mother was sitting on the toilet. She twisted round, lifted up the skirt of her green-plaid flannel nightgown, and caught a glimpse of the place her flesh was starting to rot. "Look at that," she said.

"How long has it been there?" I asked her.

"This is the first time I've seen it," my mother said. "It certainly looks painful."

The Assisted Living staff protested their innocence in the matter of the bedsore. Me, I couldn't decide which was worse—their knowing it was there and doing nothing, or their not knowing it was there.

Or *my* not knowing it was there.

On the second day of the New Year, I started looking for my mother's next doctor and her next home.

bad ancestors

Saturday morning. After a week of early risings, we've slept in, started slow. In the space between our waking and when our children emerge from their rooms upstairs, we've indulged in sex by light of day, rumpled sheets and warm skin and first sun filtered through our miniblinds—a weekend luxury. Afterward we shower. Schuyler makes his way to the kitchen to brew coffee. I light candles for his ancestors and for mine. Between our bedroom and the master bath, there's a little dressing room, two facing closets and five square feet of carpet. In one of the closets, our bovedas stand side by side, his and hers, evoking our different strains of DNA.

Schuyler's forebears are long-nosed, with egg-shaped faces. Most gaze out unsmiling from formal, frontal portraits. My kin, displayed mostly in snapshots, have squarer jaws, perkier noses, more casual expressions. Mathilde, my mother's Swedish mother, is by far the most beautiful of all the women. Except for coloring, she looks a great deal like my daughter. My father is, I suppose, the handsomest of the men. In their pictures, Schuyler's paternal grandfather and mine are both pretty boys in their twenties and look enough alike to be cousins, though Grandpa Roy, mine, seems cockier, more at home in the world than John, the frontier dentist, who looks a bit fragile and more than a bit worried. Legend has it that he chose to marry the homeliest woman in Colville, Washington.

But this is a Saturday, my house, with the washing machine swooshing away at the first load of the day, little crockery clatters coming from the kitchen, the buzz of a bass line in the walls suggesting that one of the kids is awake by now and playing rock 'n' roll. Schuyler is newly enough part of the family that he practices breakfast as an art of seduction. Today it will be waffles, the butter melted, syrup hot. When I go to the kitchen for coffee, he's mixing batter, humming softly. We kiss in passing, then I return to the bedroom to get dressed. The coffee is hot and bitter. Because I'm thick-headed from sleeping late, I pause with it in front of the boveda and turn a trancelike stare upon our collective forebears. I'm relatively new to this business of building a relationship with my ancestors, and to tell the truth, still find it baffling. I have a hard time squaring the idea of reincarnation, which I intuit to be true, with a fixed line of descent. Are these people really ancestor material, these drunks, these bankrupts, these cheated-on women, these suicides? I have spent considerable effort trying to free myself of their more destructive patterns of behavior. Perhaps, resemblances to the contrary, I was adopted, or simply dropped into this alien context from outer space.

Sighing, I tell myself I just don't get it yet, that it's not necessary to *like* one's ancestors, that with due time and application, it will get easier and make more sense. Meanwhile, there are waffles to be eaten, a house to be cleaned, kids to be caught up with after a week of scurrying. I go into the bedroom and pull on work clothes, then head to the vanity in the bathroom for mascara, which I am much too vain and pale-lashed to face the day without. As I pass through the candlelighted dressing room, though, something seizes me, no less violently for being invisible, a rush of sexual desire so strong and sudden it's almost sickening. Intensely centered in my groin, it radiates out through my whole body, a diffuse state of arousal just a neuron or two short of a whole-body orgasm. I am made weak and mightily alarmed.

To this day I cannot say for sure if I staggered to the vanity or was propelled there, draped against it. The erotic charge mounts relentlessly, and I feel sure that it does not originate from me. It seems invasive, almost abusive. I can't for the life of me shake it off, stand up straight, and walk away. Fear sits on top of eros, and I begin to tremble from the combination. When I try to call out to Schuyler, the words stick in my throat. Instead, I manage to pound on the wall. The kitchen is immediately on the other side. Schuyler should hear me. He should come. I hammer on the wall with my fists and it takes me over, a powerful, back-arching, every-cell-exploding, protracted orgasm I have done nothing to seek or stimulate. It's almost like being electrocuted. Tears stream down my cheeks. And then it's over. My body belongs to me again.

When I can walk, I go to the kitchen to ask Schuyler why he didn't come to me. He's leaning against the kitchen counter, pale as a halibut's belly.

"What the hell is going on here?" he says. "I heard some ruckus on the other side of the wall, and then boom, my legs turned to jelly and I went down on my knees."

"I needed you," I say. "Why didn't you come?"

"I couldn't," he says. "I don't know what happened. It was like I was paralyzed." He shrugs. "Maybe my blood pressure dropped really fast."

I tell Schuyler what's happened to me, and we decide I'd best call Maria in Oakland and see what she has to say. Since I scarcely know Maria, nor she me, I find it quite embarrassing to try to talk about this strange, intensely erotic experience. Is this what Freud called hysteria? Mostly, I'm afraid she'll think I'm nuts. It does sound nuts. Knowing that, I recount the tale in the most clinical language I can get my tongue around, which makes it sound even more absurd. I end by saying, "It really scared me. It was almost as if I was being raped."

Maria is silent for a moment, and when she speaks, it's kindly, in a level voice. "If the energy felt like it was coming off your boveda, then it probably was. Most people are strangers to spiritual experience. The closest thing we know is sex, so that's how we interpret it. Once you get more elevated, you'll be able to tell the difference," Maria says.

"Like chakras?" I say.

"Something like that," Maria says. "Be glad the energy is there."

And so, because I want there to be a comprehensible answer, I let myself be reassured. It was only my lack of spiritual development that made this incident seem sexual at all. Fine. I will take all the white baths Maria recommends, to raise myself up to a higher plane, and then it will feel like . . . something else?

Some tiny skeptic inside me disputes Maria's explanation, sought at long distance on scant information, says I *do* know the difference between lust and spirit, between good and evil. Some tiny skeptic continues to insist I have been ravished by invisible forces. But it is more comfortable to believe what Maria says, so I turn out the light in that room and walk away.

38

tales of Clearbrook Inn

Clearbrook Inn, in Silverdale, is the middle level of a three-tiered retirement community, a halfway station between freestanding cottages with carports and tiny lawns—Whispering Pines—and the nursing home, a big rustic A-frame called Northwoods Lodge. Clearbrook itself resembles a brand-new Ramada Inn. It has parlors and salons, two dining rooms, faux colonial wallpaper, several monumental silk flower arrangements, caged lovebirds in the lobby, a beauty parlor, even a little gift shop stocked with umbrellas and stuffed animals near the front desk. Dead center in the lower floor, there is a nurses' station, a nursing office, and a pharmacy. Long corridors recede from it in both directions, lined with doors.

It is an architectural convention of many assisted living facilities that every unit has its own kitchen, a baffling use of space since no one who needs enough assistance to live in such a place actually shops or cooks anymore. Thus my mother's studio has a tiny bed/ sitting room, a spacious kitchen, and a huge bathroom with a shower that could accommodate two wheelchairs at the same time. The back door gives onto a paved patio just big enough for two small lawn chairs and an hibachi. To foreclose the possibility of wandering, we put Anne's big old console television set square in front of the back door. You can see the nurses' station and the dining room both from my mother's front door; this, combined with the big nameplate, makes getting lost hard to do.

I am confident, having researched the alternatives, that this is the very best place my mother could be. The complex is owned and operated by a local family that's been in the elder-care business for three generations. State inspectors routinely give it the highest rating. Twice, the chef has taken first place in the cooking competition at the Kitsap County Fair. At Clearbrook, there's always at least one LPN on duty, and numerous aides. Because of the nursing home, there are always a couple of RNs just a stone's throw away, and doctors on call around the clock. There is popcorn in the afternoons, there are movies, field trips, ice-cream socials, manicures and foot care, bingo, church services, sittercise classes, sing-alongs, and even a Fourth of July picnic and parade. You can see the Olympic Mountains from the dining room. Clearbrook Inn is clean and comfortable. It smells good. It is exactly thirty minutes from my door.

My mother hates it. She hates it because it is "not Seattle." It is "just not me." The residents are not "my kind of people." There is "nothing for me here." Mostly, I think, she hates it because she feels obliged to, because she hates getting old.

the new doctor is a nurse

Moving to Silverdale meant changing doctors, too. Now, instead of being a human jigsaw puzzle composed of separate organ systems, each served by a different expert, my mother has been restored to full personhood, under the care of a Yale-trained nurse-practitioner. A single visit might last thirty or forty minutes and address everything from blood pressure to bladder control, earwax to itchy skin. Anne Ledell-Hong is an obviously intelligent woman, who practices compassion without condescension. She's tall and slender, with short red hair, paper-thin skin, and a fondness for wearing long skirts that swish prettily below the hem of her businesslike lab coat. She managed to address my mother and me as if we were a two-headed patient, distinct in our concerns about the best care that could be taken of the body for which we shared responsibility. It was she who first gave my mother the Mini Mental State Examination. The results confirmed the puzzling contradictions of her condition. While my mother had no idea what day or month or year it was, while she could remember none of a list of ten words two minutes later, her language and information-sequencing skills remained formidable. How could somebody so smart be so impaired? I suspect it was a question she often asked herself. I know it made decision-making hard.

"You know, Mrs. Thompson," Anne Ledell-Hong says, "as we get older, our bodies stop producing some of the hormones we need to function well."

Anne Thompson nods. She's eighty-five years old, scrawny, in need of a new perm. Her face still shows the effects of New Year's descent into the dark, but she listens attentively, seems comforted by the reasonable tone in which this information comes.

"Some of those hormones—serotonin, specifically—play an important role in modulating our moods. The good news is, we can replace the hormones our body's stopped making, simply by taking a pill once a day." Here, Ledell-Hong smiles at my mother. My mother smiles back politely. "I think, Mrs. Thompson, it would be a good idea for you to take that pill. I think that after a while, you'll notice a significant improvement in the quality of your life. What do you say?"

My mother's thin shoulders lift in a shrug. "Why not?" she says.

Ledell-Hong inscribes the specifics on a prescription pad. "We'll start you off on a low dose and see how it goes. We can always increase it later." Scribble, scribble. "The medication is called Zoloft," Ledell-Hong says.

"Zoloft." My mother nods.

Ledell-Hong looks at me, smiling broadly, and I grin back, acknowledging the coup. Selling an anti-depressant to a Scandinavian makes selling air conditioners to Eskimos look easy, but that's exactly what she's just done.

poison

My mother points at the intercom on the wall, beside her bed. She puts her finger to her lips. Shakes her head. Then she takes me by the hand and pulls me toward the bathroom. Once we're both inside, she closes the door.

"They listen," she says.

"Do you really think so?"

"I know so," my mother says. "That's why we have to talk in here." She flushes the toilet, and while the water roars away, leans close. "They're trying to poison me," she says.

"Really? How do you know?"

"If I take their pills, I get sick to my stomach."

"Maybe you have a touch of the flu."

My mother flushes the toilet again. "It's those pills. I know it. You have to get me out of here before they kill me."

"They make their money looking after you. Why would they want to kill you?"

"You don't live here. I do."

"True enough. But I think they're taking pretty good care of you, Mom. You look good. You seem chipper."

"Poison," my mother says.

Paranoia. That's what I say to myself.

My mother flushes the toilet again; then we move from the bathroom to her sitting room and settle in, she in her armchair, I on the edge of her brass bed. "So, what have you been up to?" my mother asks me. Her voice is unnaturally bright. I must look surprised, because she points at the intercom. Go on, talk.

"Same old, same old," I say. "How about you? Are they treating you well?"

"I can't complain." My mother says it to the speaker, not to me.

For several weeks, I believed my mother was spinning out. Way out. If I didn't do her laundry, I might never have seen the truth. Pair after pair of her panties was soiled when I put them in the machine. She really did have diarrhea. I spoke to the nurses at Clearbrook, and learned that especially in the evenings, my mother complained of stomach upsets. Armed with this information, I called the nurse-practitioner. "She thinks her pills are causing it," I said.

"She's probably right," Ledell-Hong said. "You know the memory drug we put her on? Upset stomach is a well-documented side effect of Aricept."

"Bingo," I said.

"Have you noticed any improvement in her memory?"

"Not really."

"Let's stop poisoning her then, shall we?" Ledell-Hong said.

the nanolife of Jan

One day, I yelled at my mother. It was on the telephone. I'd called to tell her I'd be coming to see her later that afternoon. We'd barely gotten hello out of the way before she started to complain. Something in me snapped and I started reeling off home truths. In my mother's family, the tolerance for home truths hovers right around zero. The times I'd risked them before, occasions it's possible to tally on fewer than the fingers of one hand, my mother treated me as if I were a dangerous lunatic, with the result that the shelf-life of my anger is about forty seconds. After that, it turns to guilt. I apologize.

That day, I did not apologize.

Everything I said to my mother was true. That she was no longer capable of living alone. That another month at the Grosvenor House would most likely have killed her. That she never took advantage of the city when she lived there. That Schuyler and I and our kids were the only visitors she ever had, so visiting her might just as well be convenient for us. That Clearbrook Inn was a nice place. We were nice people. That a little gratitude might be in order.

Finally, I told her if she really wanted to live in an apartment in Seattle that badly, I would take her to look for one. I would help her move into it. And then I would wash my hands of her. Forty seconds later, I apologized for yelling.

Then I took a deep breath and waited for things to escalate.

In the days when she was sure of her power, my mother would have hung up on me. I would have had to call her back, perhaps several times, before things were smoothed over. Now she simply stayed on the line, silent. I could hear her breathing. I told her I loved her. I told her to gather up all her dirty clothes because I was coming to see her later that afternoon. Instead of sulking, instead of telling me not to come, she didn't want to see me if I was going to be "like this," all she said was, "What time do you think you'll get here?" The sweetness of winning a round at last was diminished, somehow, by the resignation in my mother's voice.

By the time I arrived in Silverdale that afternoon, my mother had made a creative readjustment of reality. "I made a terrible mistake moving here," she announced. "It was a bad decision. I have nobody to blame but myself, I know that. I can't imagine what I was thinking." Here she paused for a moment, then met my eyes. "You will help me correct it, won't you?"

Without missing more than half a beat, I took up my part. "Well, sure, but I'm afraid it won't happen fast. We'll have to do some thorough research. Rents are very high in Seattle right now, availability's low, and you wouldn't want to get into the wrong building and have to move all over again."

"I have a vague recollection of Jan telling me I have an apartment waiting for me in Seattle," my mother said. "What do you know about that?"

"First I've heard of it," I said. "You had an apartment at the Grosvenor House, but we had to give that up."

"I'm sure Jan said I had a nice apartment."

"Tell me who Jan is, Mom," I said.

"Oh, you remember Jan. I'm sure you met. Very nice woman. Sort of a . . . well, an ombudswoman. You know, for people like me."

"Oh," I said. "Jan."

"I'm sure she'd help us, if we could get in touch with her."

"Do you have an address or phone number for her, Mom?"

"Well, no. I don't. But I'm sure you can find her if you try. You met her once, I'm sure."

"I'll see if I can't track her down. Okay?"

And so, the quest for Jan began that day. It took me quite a while to find her number, and once I did, it turned out she'd gone away on a long trip to Europe. It would be several months before we could expect her to be in touch. Every time my mother started to freak out, I reminded her that things were underway, Jan would surely be in touch when she got back from Europe, and she was comforted by that. Over time, Jan became Fran, and she grew in her power to take things over, to make them right, until I was pretty sure that in my mom's cosmology, Jan/Fran stood for God. I even considered writing my mother a letter from Jan, but then decided that while it was okay to spin tales orally, to create false evidence would be going too far. Like any good imaginary friend, Jan lived long enough to do her work, giving Anne hope while she settled into yet another set of strange surroundings, adjusted to new daily rhythms and a different set of medications.

And then she disappeared.

mall rats and report cards

If I sat with my mother in her room, she would inevitably begin to bitch and moan. If I put on her lipstick and her coat and took her out, she was content, her complaints swept away by the power of the incoming scene. Everything she saw was of interest—the shape and textures of the clouds, the lushness of the roadside trees, the colors of the cars we passed. Sometimes we'd bring her home to Bainbridge, most often for Sunday dinner; that was a half-day excursion, and much as she derided her apartment when she was there, a few hours with us and she was quite eager to get back. Sometimes, she even skipped dessert. The Silverdale Mall was always good for a walk, some people-watching, a cup of coffee, and a Cinnabon. Even if she'd just finished eating a full meal, my mother could always put away a Cinnabon. We became regulars at the Red Robin and the Brew Pub and the Pancake House.

The foolproof Annie outing, the one I always smile remembering, was Costco. Every few weeks, we'd go there to stock up on something wholesale—coffee, or toilet paper, or toothpaste, or printer ribbons— and my mom was always game to go along. She liked to push the cart because it steadied her, and we made our way from aisle to aisle to-gether, filling up on free samples. She who had always found small children noisy, messy, and annoying was now powerfully drawn to them. Anne made faces and flirted with toddlers in their carts; she bent over to ask them questions. She exclaimed loudly at overweight, over-made-up, or weirdly dressed people—"Will you look at that!" For her, it was like a trip to the circus every time, one that always ended with a root beer and a Polish hotdog.

My mother loved our field trips for themselves, and for the status they brought her at Clearbrook. To have a single visitor was good. Two visitors was doubly so, especially if one was a man. Best of all were young people, children or teens. Young visitors, especially if they were polite and friendly, were equal to or better than getting off the premises entirely. My son was always willing to take his grandma's arm, to escort her through the lobby with theatrically good manners. My mother loved to be seen leaving, especially in his company. She loved to be signed out in the big book at the nurses' station, where next to her name appeared the date, her destination, the person she was with, when she left, and finally, what time she was delivered safely back. I learned from the nurses that she would sometimes pore over the sign-out book, reviewing excursions she couldn't remember taking, comparing how often she'd been taken out versus how many times her neighbors had. Sometimes, I must confess, I scanned those pages, too. No one gives you a report card when you're caring for a parent; those entries became something like an attendance record. If my mom's name appeared a couple of times on every page, then I was being a good daughter. My lapses were instantly apparent.

the laundress

Why did I insist on doing my mother's laundry all that time?

It saved a bit of money, yes, but an exceedingly small amount compared to the other services we subscribed to on her behalf. If there were to be a sticking point, surely, you'd think, that would have been it. I can easily imagine a daughter in an alternate universe saying, "I am a professional woman, not a laundress; my mother can afford to hire someone besides me to wash her dirty underwear." To have sloughed off that small service, though, would have made me someone I did not wish to be.

I would have been someone who left the dirty work for someone else. I would have thought, implicitly, that I was better than the woman I hired to wash those clothes and linens in my stead. I would probably have been exploiting a woman from the Third World, where females lack the opportunities for education and employment that I've had. I would have been avoiding quotidian commitment; clean clothes get dirty, again and again. To do the laundry is not a one-time thing. I would have been saying that having clean clothes was a matter of small importance. And I would have foreclosed the possibility of expressing my love, my loyalty, in a very straightforward, uncomplicated way.

From time to time, I resented how much my mother weighed upon my life, but I never resented doing her laundry. That it was important to me to do it suggests that much as I was absorbed in caring for my mother, I was still in some ways Ethel's girl.

busted

Why didn't my mother answer the phone?

It had been several years since she'd initiated a call. Even with automatic dialing—just push number one—the task was either beyond performing, or beyond her wanting to. But she had always been quick to pick up the phone when I called her. Now, though, it simply rang and rang. I made sure I wasn't calling at mealtimes, when she'd be in the dining room, and in case she was in the bathroom, I always tried again later. After a couple of days of this, I called the nurses' station and asked Kathy to see if my mother was all right.

"She seems to be doing just fine," Kathy told me.

I asked her if she'd check and see if my mother's phone was in working order. I pictured it knocked off the hook. I pictured it broken. At least I was no longer picturing my mother in the same sorry state. A few minutes later, Kathy called me back on my mother's working phone.

"Have you noticed any deterioration in her hearing?" I asked. "Maybe she just can't hear the phone."

Kathy was a big woman, with a hearty laugh. It boomed across the line. "She can't hear the phone because she isn't in her room," Kathy said. "She's hanging out. Two nights ago, when we had the piano player in, your mother bellied right up to the piano and sang every song. She even danced a little. It must have been eleven-thirty before she went to bed."

"My mother?" I said.

"Uh-huh. All of a sudden, she's quite the social butterfly."

"Wow," I said. "Wow. She still tells me how unhappy she is. How much she wants to move."

Kathy laughed again. "I don't think so," she said. "Maybe she just says that to, you know, save face."

"Singing, huh?"

"All the old songs. For hours and hours."

The next time I went to visit, my mother warbled a verse or two of "Clementine" in a creditable if slightly shopworn soprano. Her voice rising up, the sparkle in her eye, told me what Kathy said was true. My mother had two lives. One was fun. The other was a prison built of expectations.

39

bathtime

My mother never much liked water and senile people don't much like water, and my mother senile was quite adamant about not bathing. Even senile, weighing in at a hundred and twenty pounds, my mother was formidable enough to hold a whole army of lazy LPNs at bay. Winter did not betray their inattention, but the first truly warm spring day released all the bodily odors pent up in Anne's clothing and her bedding and her furniture, on her skin and in her hair. It didn't bother her a whit, since her sense of smell had gone south before her short-term memory did, around age eighty, but when the sun shone on my mother's room all afternoon, the air grew so thick it made your eyes water. Excursions by car required having the windows rolled down and the heater cranked up high. Every time we bought her a bale of toilet paper at Costco, we tossed in a six-pack of room deodorizers, the kind that start out about the consistency of jellied cranberry sauce and slowly wizen up. Every load of wash came reeking to my house and went back lemon fresh. A week later, it all stank again. The level never seemed to go down on the four-dozen pack of Depends we laid in for her, although the carpet in her room was often dotted with mysterious missile-shaped wads of toilet paper, as if Hansel and Gretel had passed through and used what came to hand to leave a trail.

Naturally we—Schuyler, the kids, and I—traded looks when we were with her and smelly granny jokes when we were not. It sounds cruel, maybe, but it helped, letting us find entertainment value in a situation that otherwise might well have been pure burden. What *was* burdensome, after a while, was paying a monthly bill that listed two showers a week as services rendered when the inmate in question was as ripe as the dump on an August afternoon. My longer-than-it-should-have-been silence in the matter came from the lack of viable alternatives. If Clearbrook decided my mother was "too far gone" to live there, "independently," the next step was a nursing home. A regimented, no-privacy, food's-lousy, smelly, abandon-hope-all-ye-who-enter-here nursing home where toothless people in wheelchairs drool and mutter all day long. Maybe nursing homes aren't really like that, but that *was* the stereotype, and no matter how impaired my mother might seem to be, she wasn't ready for *that*. My reluctance to rock the boat resulted in a couple months of stalemate with the Clearbrook staff. I'd say, "About those showers . . ." and they'd say something like, "Oh, your mom wasn't feeling well on Thursday so we didn't have one. I'll make certain sure she has one Saturday."

Saturday came and went. The stench remained.

Eventually my mother tanked.

First she stopped leaving her room. Then she stopped leaving her bed. Her color went bad and she was more confused than ever. She picked at the trays of food the nurses brought her. Did she hurt somewhere? Did she have any idea what was wrong? She did not. Fortunately, our nurse-practitioner recognized the signs. What the Clearbrook staff surmised might have been a little stroke was nothing more nor less than that bane of the not-quite-daisy-fresh geriatric, a bladder infection. A couple of days on antibiotics and the world looked bright again. On my next visit, Kathy pulled me aside.

"You know, your ma won't take a shower." Kathy was on her second or third husband, with most of her five kids grown up and gone. Big and raw-boned, her hair dyed an in-your-face shade of red, she looked tough as a retired Roller Derby queen, which didn't keep her from collecting Beanie Babies or being remarkably gentle with her charges.

"I figured," I said. "I talked to the other nurse about it."

"It's not like I couldn't *throw* her in the shower," Kathy said. "I'm strong enough, but I'm pretty sure that's illegal."

"Probably," I said.

"So all's we do is ask her twice a week would she like a shower, and on a good day she says no or if she's feeling ornery go fuck yourself. You shouldn't be paying for something that doesn't happen. If I was you, I'd cancel the service and shower her yourself."

"Ahhhh."

"Some of the other families do that," Kathy said. "Please don't tell my boss I told you."

I promised I would not.

I spent a long time in the Bed and Bath section of J. C. Penney, looking for just the right stuff. If I fell short on moral authority, I figured an appeal to the senses might make up for it. Sea-foam green, shell pink, or moon-silver blue? I went back and forth for a long time before I picked the blue for her giant, deep-nap bath towel. Peach for the foaming bath gel and matching lotion. Pale yellow for the tulle scrubber. Frank Sinatra's greatest hits was the best I could do for the soundtrack. They don't make CDs of Bing Crosby or Sons of the Pioneers, and I was not about to sink to Kenny G. As I shopped, I murmured to myself, I'm sure of it. *I bathe my mother now.*

"Doctor says I can't get wet," my mother said.

"Doctor said you couldn't get your *stitches* wet, but you got your stitches out six months ago."

"What doctor are you talking about?" my mother said.

"Same one you are. The one who said you have to take a shower at least once a week or you'll get sick."

"Oh, I don't believe that," my mother said.

"Believe it. Besides, you're starting to smell."

My mother sniffed the same air that was gagging me. "I don't smell anything."

"I know. You'll have to trust me on this one. Let's get your clothes off now."

I turned her thermostat up high so she wouldn't feel cold and started at the top, unbuttoning her purple blouse. Reflexively, she started to unbutton from the bottom. "What a team," I said.

"You better draw the drapes," my mother said. "I don't want that fellow out there in the yard seeing me naked."

In the yard two fat crows terrorized a smattering of sparrows. Creamy rhododendron blossoms with bruised hearts nodded in a light breeze. No man that I could see, but I closed the drapes anyway. My mother's naked body had lost skirmishes with gravity and drought. After two lumpectomies, one of her breasts was smaller than the other, the nipple off center. The scar from the arterial bypass was so old and smooth it looked like polished wood. What seemed most intimate were the few coarse black hairs that sprouted from my mother's flesh, vestigial, symbolic hair in the places a younger woman would have lusty tufts.

Once she was naked, Anne grew submissive. She waited patiently while I fiddled with the shower dials. "I'm going for the temperature of baby formula," I told her. "Why don't you see how that feels now?"

Dutifully, my mother stepped into the shower, but when the warm spray hit her skin, she recoiled from it as if she were in pain. The tulle scrubber with its load of peach bath gel didn't even have to touch her skin to make her flinch.

"Does that hurt you, Mom?" I asked.

My mother shook her head no. "I just don't like it much, is all."

In the other room, Frank Sinatra crooned a romantic forties ballad my mother seemed to have heard before. I raised a deep lather on the scrubber, started at my mother's neck, and worked my way down, making little soapy circles all over her old skin.

"Armies up," I chanted, lifting first right, then left arms up from her sides so I could scrub the pits.

"Boobies." One by one, I lifted up the flaps of her breasts and soaped the trough of flesh beneath.

"Bunnies." Same with her buttocks, where each deflated cheek hung down.

"Gyny! Ahhhhhh." I slid the scrubber back and forth between my mother's legs, frothing her stringy little flag of pubic hair. At that, she giggled.

"Legs," I exclaimed, humming a little leg-washing song, the same one I'd sung as I bathed my children so many years before. My mother's legs were thin and red, the skin taut and shiny. Down the inside of each one ran a long, thin white line, scars that commemorated where they'd taken veins to heal her heart. Her feet were swollen, almost purple. I made her lift each one up so I could wash the bottom. "That tickles," my mother said.

"And now, the face," I cried.

"Oh no," my mother said. "Not the face." She ducked away from the scrubber.

"Must," I said. "Absolutely have to." I struck quickly, preempting argument. My mother scrunched her face up, sputtering. She looked about four. The shower head was attached to a long hose. I took it down from the stall wall and sprayed my mother's shower cap first. "Rain on the roof." I got her face, fast—she swore at me—and then worked my way down, erasing my soapy tracks. No stink, I figured, could survive my brisk attack. Soon she was swaddled in her new blue towel. I patted her dry.

"Lotion!" I rubbed it warm in my hands first, then slathered it all over her thirsty pink skin. "That wasn't so bad, now, was it?" My mother allowed as how it was not. Quietly, in my heart, I concurred.

Somehow, I'd kicked into my manic-mama energy and found out it worked with elders as well as toddlers. I was as pleased with my success in this as in anything else I'd done the last few years, gloating a bit and telling myself those nurses were wusses. Fifteen minutes and my mother smelled sweet as a peach orchard in August, when the fruit hangs plump and juicy.

Then I took off her shower cap, and her hair released its cache of fumes.

"Mom, I'm going to make you another appointment in the beauty shop. Promise me this time you'll go with the lady when she comes to get you."

"What lady?" my mother said.

"Tell you what: I'll have her call me when she comes to get you. Then I can tell you it's okay to go with her."

Not for the first time, I showed my mother how to secure a Depends before I put her panties on. Then I dressed her in clean clothes, brushed her hair, put on her lipstick, and led her out to the nurses' station, just in time for evening meds and dinner. Kathy took in the improvement and gave me two thumbs up. A tiny lady with watery blue eyes said, "You look so pretty, Anne. Did you do something different with your hair?"

My mother pointed at me. "She did it." I gave her a big kiss and, as the residents made their way to their assigned seats in the dining room, eased away.

The lovebirds in the lobby were quarreling over a little tray of birdseed. I felt as if Anne and I had just passed an important test. I was optimistic about my ability to keep my mother clean. The only problem was that half-hour of time and space between her door and mine.

story's last stand

The sixteen months Anne lived at Clearbrook Inn were the swan song of the raconteur. During them, she told a different set of stories than she ever had before. Characters who once figured prominently no longer had even walk-on parts. Incidents once central to her personal mythology went untold. Her literal biography became subject to wishful revisions. There was the occasional breathtaking flash of candor.

As ever, I was my mother's most devoted audience. New was the urgency of my listening, the awareness that sooner than later, the source would dry up and the stories cease to flow, perhaps before I'd come to understand who my mother was and how she came to be that way, or how that made me *me*.

in memory of Olaf

For about a year, my mother told this story almost incessantly, sometimes half a dozen times in a few hours' visit.

"I wanted to do something with my life that would have made my father proud of me. He was an engineer, but I wasn't good enough in math and science to follow in his footsteps. Then I remembered that he thought very highly of his attorney, and I decided I could do that. So I went to law school and became a lawyer."

Add to my mother's story these shards of fact. My Aunt Adeline wanted to be a nurse. My Aunt Olga wanted to teach high school. My grandfather refused them both, feeling that a daughter who had to work brought shame upon her father. His sons, he felt, should learn as he had, from experience, and not from school. My mother was the only one of his eight children to go to college, that because he was already dead.

improving Howard

Only one story with my father in it survived into my mother's dementia, and for a while she told it frequently. The story had to do with a trip my parents took by boat. Their destination was a resort motel, where they secured the last available room. Soon after dark, a knock came at the door, fellow travelers seeking a place to stay for the night. As luck would have it, these were people my parents already knew, a former Democratic governor and his wife. My folks shared their lodgings. A good time was had by all.

Why would this oddly meaningless anecdote survive so long while so many others more pointed or polished fell away? At first I thought it was because of the status of the other couple, a harmless bit of snobbism. Then one day, Anne embellished the story just a little bit, referring to the bottle of whiskey the other couple brought with them, how quickly the other husband finished it off. In fact, as I recalled the real event, the trip had turned into a roaring two-couple boozing binge. "You must have had quite the hangovers," I said.

My mother cocked her head in the birdlike way she had in her eighties and said, "Well, I suppose M. did, but you know, Howard and I never drank much. I was always grateful for that."

For a moment, I was too amazed even to breathe. With just two sentences, my mother had completely rewritten the past we all had shared, erasing its central fact. At first I wanted to argue with her, to insist on the validity of my own suffering, the nobility of hers. Then, all at once, I appreciated the power and the beauty of her revisions. I laughed instead.

Emmett does not regret

"Emmett was sitting cross-legged on top of the woodbox in the kitchen, like he always did. Do you remember? Olga had brought him a letter from the post office, from Mary Dean. Mary Dean was a friend of Olga's, and she was very much in love with Emmett. I suppose we all assumed they'd get married one day.

"Anyway, Emmett opened his letter and he read it through once to himself, and then he read it out loud to us. 'Dear Emmett, I am writing to tell you that I have gotten engaged to marry Cyrus Holmes. I have waited for you for a long time, but I cannot wait forever. I wish you all the best. Mary Dean.'

"Emmett folded up the letter and put it in his pocket. Then he gave us one of his big Emmett grins. He said, 'Well, she may come to regret that one day, but I never will.'"

As my father passed out of my mother's conversation in her last years, her brother Emmett took up the vacant space. "He was a great guy," she'd say. "He was a terrible tease. Liked to get people's goat. Handsome, too. We always had so much fun." He was clearly her favorite brother, probably her favorite man, and dementia brought him close, even though he'd been dead for thirty years by then. While my mother told the story of the letter and the woodbox verbatim, with the frequency and precision of a prayer, I had the sense that its meaning shifted over time. At first, it was the story the family told about why such an attractive, charming man as Emmett, who so liked children, remained a bachelor all his days, the implication being that Mary Dean was the one, irreplaceable "love of his life." Over time and many tellings, as a certain truth-telling impishness came upon my mom, other meanings crept in. Anne was clearly quite pleased, for example, that her favorite brother had not married Mary Dean. She began to add the suspicion that he must have had one or more bang-up love affairs while he was in Panama, and left all that behind him when he returned home. Ever thereafter, he lived at home, or sometimes with his old friend Johnny in his cabin by the river.

In the spring of 1998, my mother told the letter story as reflexively as you hum a song that's stuck in your head. In early April of that year, just days after his fourteenth birthday, my son shared with the immediate family the news that he was sexually attracted to boys, not girls. Whatever adjustments of attitude or expectation this confidence required of the rest of us were small compared to the peace that acknowledging his true nature brought to my son. He is a brave and decisive human being. For me, a mother, his coming out required an inescapable period of mourning for the children he would not have, a hardwired emotional response I suspect occurs whenever a child drops out of the gene pool, for whatever reason. In the wake of the death of Matthew Shepard, I had to deal with real fear for my child at the hands of a barbaric culture. Finally, I had to think about what makes a person straight or gay.

In the absence of hard truth, this kind of thinking is a riff played among facts, theories, memory, history, intuition. Thus engaged, I realized that Ian had always been himself, and at some deep level, I had always known he was probably gay. While he'd grown up without a father on the premises, he spent one weekend a month with his dad, and there were always male friends, teachers, and relatives abundant in his world, none who abused him. I faithfully enrolled him in gymnastics, soccer, baseball, basketball, track, and swim team and he faithfully showed up, until he finally persuaded me to get off his case and let him take a pottery class instead of a sport one spring. While we were close, I do not believe I was ever controlling or curtailed his freedom to take risks. He has never been timid or lacked confidence. While I did my best to forbid both my children war toys, I never discouraged competition, rowdiness, or otherwise character-building bad behavior. None of the usual theoretical constructs seemed to apply. I don't believe I made my son gay.

At this point, I dived into the literature, ordering so many books from Amazon that their database will ever after offer me the latest gay titles when I log on. I read history and fiction and personal testimony. I studied photographic albums of male friendships over the decades. I tried to pry open my own mind and my own heart, to root out the homophobic shadows that lingered there. I learned that to fully accept one's gay child, one must come out oneself. I began to wonder, finally, just why a human being's sexual preference is anyone's business but his or her own. My son passed through a phase of intense politicization, when "gay" was the first adjective he used to describe himself. In time this passed, and all his other, unique attributes superseded sexual orientation as the hallmarks of self-definition, but for a necessary while, we were a slogan-chanting, rainbow-wearing household, and proud of it.

In light of this new information, I began to look at my family in new ways, and found among them a bevy of bachelors, from my grandpa's three unmarried brothers to my uncles Oscar and Emmett, and so unto my children's generation, with its odd-duck cousins who don't appear to date and rarely show up at family affairs.

I found pictures of those uncles as young teenagers, looking impossibly girlish among the rough hands in their father's construction camps. I found a picture of my Uncle Oscar, the suicide, and his army buddy George in full doughboy regalia, heads touching and hands joined, their smiles sweet, their eyes tender, the affection between them undisguised. For that matter, I found a formal portrait of my Grandpa Roy, the only child of two schoolteachers turned subsistence farmers, in which at age six or seven he is got up in a satin dress with lace cuffs, his hair dressed in sausage curls well past his shoulders and tied up with a pretty bow. When my son cast a glance at a photo of his charming Uncle Emmett, as a twentysomething in dandy duds, he exclaimed without coaching, "He is *so* gay." Eventually, I came to speculate that, in a family unwilling to be candid even about its drinking habits, a number of my male relations lived or were living half or hidden lives.

All through this time, my mother continued to tell and retell the story of Mary Dean. After a while, I couldn't resist asking questions that touched on sexual preference. She would consider for a moment and then deny, always invoking the mysterious Panama affair.

The truth of these lives is beyond my knowing. But I hope that my bachelor uncles, whomever they fancied, knew what it feels like to love and to be loved.

the pretty baby

"I could think of no more dismal way to spend a summer than to haul a kid around the city, park to park, wading pool to wading pool. Phooey. I refused to do it. That's what led us to buy the lot on Bainbridge and build the beach house, so I wouldn't have to be a city mom," my mother says.

She's sitting in the front seat with Schuyler and I'm in back, half daydreaming, half listening in. I'm pretty sure Anne's forgotten I'm in the car.

"It must have been fun, though, having a pretty little girl to play with," Schuyler says.

Anne is silent for a moment. When she speaks, it's low and slow, in a confidential voice one rarely hears from her. "To tell you the truth," she says, "it was really hard for me. I'd take the baby out in her stroller, and strangers would stop me. Oh, such pretty red hair. What a sweet thing. Koochie-koo. They made a terrible fuss. I couldn't help but resent it." My mother was quiet for a moment. Then she said, "I did my best to hide it, you know, to not act like I was jealous. I think I did a pretty good job. But it was damn hard sometimes."

This is less a story than a confession, really. I heard it only once.

Anna and Mathilde

This is a story my mother never told.

My cousin Orky shows me a picture of our great-grandmother, Anna. It makes no sense to me, how this thick-waisted woman with her crude features could beget Mathilde, my grandmother, creature of high cheekbones and tiny ears, clear brow and almond eyes. Anna's eyes are deep, downward slashes, her forehead low and sloped. She looks a lot like a monkey. Genes play tricks, I know—all I have of Mathilde is her willowy height, of my mother, less even than that, although my daughter resembles both—but the disparity between Anna and Mathilde almost defies belief. To my cousin Orky, I say, "What must it have been like for her, to be an ugly woman with such a beautiful daughter?"

Orky answers me with the answer she's puzzled out for herself. "Anna had a hard life," she says. "Her husbands beat her. She probably looked a lot different before that happened."

"Husbands?" I say. This is the first I've heard of *husbands.*

"Well," Orky says, "I guess she wasn't really ever married to the first one, even though she had a son by him."

"Wow." It's the best I can do in light of this news.

"Her children had different fathers. Mathilde's father took in Anna and her son."

"That was nice," I say, but Orky says, "I don't think so. He was a violent man. First her son left Sweden for Montana, and when he sent home enough money, Mathilde followed. That's where she met Olaf, our grandfather, you know. She was a chambermaid in the hotel. He worked for the railroad."

I stare at simian Anna, trying to imagine her life. Orky turns the album page, and I see a small, old-fashioned garden, some of it shaded by a big old tree. "Ingegerd says that Anna used to sit under that tree and cry for Mathilde."

My own beautiful daughter has recently left home to seek her further education. There are days that I, too, sit and weep from missing her.

"They wrote letters," Orky goes on, "but they never saw each other on this earth again. Olaf told Mathilde that he would pay her passage home to Sweden to see her mother, but if she went, not to bother coming back."

"What about after he died?"

"Anna was already gone," Orky says.

41

communication technologies

Trance possession is the most whimsical, least predictable interface between humans and orishas. Some days, Ochun has nothing to say to you, even though she might spend ten minutes counseling your neighbor. If you're agile and determined, you might manage to salute her anyway and receive a blessing, or a hug, in return. Or maybe she says a mouthful, but because she's speaking Spanish and you don't, you receive only a small part of her message. Then there's the question of talking back. While your godmother assures you it's okay to ask questions, your tongue may falter at the very thought. Finally, the presence of an orisha in the flesh, mounted on the head of a priest, is hardly an everyday occurrence. Fortunately, there are other, more reliably accessible ways of conversing with God.

Obi is a do-it-yourself, daily-if-you-need-to divination system performed with four pieces of coconut. Anyone who works with his or her ancestors can use it to consult with them; anyone who has undergone the preliminary initiation of receiving warriors can use obi to apply for advice to Eleggua who is keeper of the crossroads, opener of the way, the orisha who carries messages between human beings and the higher forms of God. The process of divination begins in prayer, to focus attention and to invoke the aid of a whole community of spiritual forebears that stretches back beyond the remembrance of specific individuals.

Questions addressed to orishas or to ancestors through this oracle must be formulated in such a way that they can be answered yes or no. And in that seeming simplicity lies the great sophistication of the system. To reduce a complicated, messy human situation, rife with nuance, possibility, temptation, mixed motives, and unforeseeable outcome, to a binary operation requires clear vision and astute analysis. In stating one's problem, one may well resolve it. If uncertainty remains, the entity you have invoked will give you advice along a continuum that ranges from absolute *yes* to *don't even go there*. To an experienced diviner, the patterns in which the coconut pieces fall yield as much information as whether they land with light or dark side showing. Not only does obi prognosticate outcome, it gives the one who consults it a way to determine if there are things she can do to make things turn out the way she wants them to.

I am a baby in the uses of this oracle.

If obi is quotidian, diloggun is cosmic. Through it, 16 cowrie shells invoke 256 odu, or fixed bits of living wisdom, each of which becomes mutable in the instant of falling, each of which expresses a subtly different relationship between the client and his fate. Each of the 256 odu may arrive in one's life with blessings, with difficulties, or with omens of impending doom. Different orishas speak in different odu, and it is from those orishas, once they are identified, that help is sought.

Help comes in the form of ebo, a prescription given the client by the diviner, which may consist of a simple gift to the spiritual entity involved, perhaps an offering made at the place in the natural world where that entity dwells. One may be required to make something, to cook something, to change or communicate or to sacrifice something. Ebos are endlessly diverse, detailed, more or less demanding. They require action as well as thought. To compare them to the expiations of other religions is to taint them with guilt and other alien assumptions. Ebo is less about penance than the restoration of balance among the forces of the planet, divinity, society, and self.

If the brilliance of obi lies in the fostering of clear thinking and daily give-and-take communication, the gift of diloggun is the engagement of intention, the movement of energy. It is prayer that carries the seed of its own answer, the objective correlative in action. The oracle itself chooses its practitioners, and uses their insight and intuition to make its messages eloquent for a particular client in a particular culture at a particular moment in history.

The effect of ebo is both magical and psychological. Every diloggun reading I have had, every ebo I have performed has had the impact on my life and psyche of at least six months of talk therapy with a good counselor. In my first reading ever, I was told to clear out all the accumulated stuff and junk of my past, in order to make room for Schuyler. Numerous trips to the dump and Goodwill later, my lover fit comfortably into my psyche and my condo, and I had a clean garage for at least three weeks.

42

initiation

When I saw that Schuyler and I would be together for a long time, I sent an email to Maria, his godmother, whom I had never met. I introduced myself as the woman with two children she and Rosi had seen coming into Schuyler's life. Now I was here. My name was Joyce. I said I didn't know if his spiritual path would ever be mine, but that I would always respect it and would do nothing to hinder him on his way. This seemed like the proper, courteous thing to do. Whether I did it for Maria's benefit, or for my own, to speak out loud both my acceptance and my intention, I can't be sure. She responded promptly and tersely, with her blessings. The email was signed *Madrina*.

Even in an impersonal electronic font on a computer screen, that word—godmother—was enough to incite prickles of longing and fear. Any word that flirts with *mother*, with all the things a mother is and is not supposed to be, is almost like a living thing to me, irresistibly appealing, but dangerous, too—a wolf cub with small sharp teeth, an unpredictable nature. It is a word that calls up all of my defenses, then scurries past them. Put the words *god* and *mother* together and you hold my heart in your hands. I have found no way to protect myself from my need. In the end, all I can do is have faith in my own resilience.

It took me four years to decide.

I flew into Oakland from LA on a Sunday morning in June. My rental car was waiting for me, but over and over, my credit card was rejected. The card had been issued by my local bank, which offered no customer service on a weekend to make things right. Schuyler suggested I call his sister in San Francisco to see if she wouldn't put the car on her card. She made a counteroffer. If I could get to their house from the airport, they'd loan me their second car for the twenty-four hours I was going to be around. Her husband, Michael, met me at the BART station nearest their home.

What was I doing in Oakland, anyhow? he asked.

I told him I'd come for an initiation.

"In that religion Schuyler belongs to? In Santeria?"

"Uh-huh. But not because he belongs. Because I want to."

"It's paganism," Michael said. "Isn't it?"

"It's an ancient and very wise spiritual practice. It makes sense to me in a way no other religion ever has."

"You didn't answer my question. Is it pagan or not?"

"Earth-based," I said.

"Not Christian," Michael said. "Without Christ, there can be no salvation."

"There are many roads to God," I said.

Michael kept smiling, but he shook his head. When he spoke, his voice was stern. "We can't both be right," he said. "There is only one Way."

As a good Christian and a good brother-in-law and a good host, Michael let me eat lunch at his table, with his family. He let me borrow his car. The only thing he denied me was admission to the heaven he planned to attain himself.

The next day, when I came back to return their car dressed all in white, Michael was home with a head cold, but he did not choose to leave his room.

In our ile, the first initiation is the receiving of elekes, cleaned and blessed beaded necklaces that invoke the protection of the orishas whom they represent. By giving me elekes, Maria was committing herself to me as madrina, Rosi as ayubona (a kind of spiritual mid-wife), and I to them as godchild, a reciprocal commitment meant to be at least as durable as a contemporary marriage. All this was understood, agreed upon before the ceremony made it formal. What was undecided until the day itself was the response of the orishas to my petition. Without the assent of Oggun, the ceremony could not proceed. Once that was given, it remained to ascertain which of the orishas would step forward to take me under wing for the next phase of my spiritual journey. Two other initiates went before me. When it was my turn at last, I prostrated myself on a straw mat before Maria's Oggun.

"Tell him who you are and why you want your elekes," Maria instructed, handing me the rattle that would get and hold Oggun's attention while I had business with him.

I was unprepared for the question. Not that I hadn't thought, more or less exhaustively, about my motivations. It was just that I hadn't expected to have to say it all out loud. If Maria had been standing just a couple of feet farther away, clearly out of earshot, I would have had less trouble being candid with Oggun. As far as I knew my own heart and mind, what I wanted most was to develop my own spiritual and psychic powers. I wanted to know more about those invisible, unnamed creatures I had long sensed were stirring in and around me. I wanted to know more about reality and the nature of time. I wanted to bring the shadows into clear focus. I wanted to live in daily commerce with the divine. Most of all, I wanted teachers to show me the way. It seemed like a lot to want.

I definitely didn't want Maria to think I was prideful or grandiose. To avoid offending her, I told Oggun a bunch of namby-pamby, meant-to-be self effacing stuff, not too much different from what I parroted back to the starchy-collared priest in my Episcopal confirmation class when I was twelve, and hoped that, being orisha, he would be able to read between the lines. I wanted to be a better person. I wanted to make a better world. Blah blah blah. Maria cleared her throat. I wrapped it up. Then she threw obi. I might have been blessed, or I might have been spurned. As it was, the letter was itawa meji, with its promise of struggle. Possible but difficult—orisha's equivalent of a cosmic shrug. I couldn't help but take it as an editorial comment on my evasions. Again, at lightning speed, Maria prayed in Lucumi. She threw the coconut again. She muttered. Threw yet again. Made a noise deep in her throat. Then she scooped up the pieces of coconut and turned to me.

"Omo Obatala," she said. Obatala's child. There was something like apology in her round black eyes. "I was surprised, too," she said.

Ochun had not stepped forward. Instead of the mother's embrace I had halfway expected, I came into the keeping of a wise and distant king whom I didn't know or understand at all.

Obatala was put in charge of creating the world. One day when he was making people, he drank too much palm wine. Obatala loved his palm wine. The people he created in his cups were broken, missing parts, or badly made. When Obatala sobered up and saw what he had done, he was very sorry. He stopped drinking wine, and ever after he has treated his imperfect creations with great tenderness. Thus it is said that the deformed, the crippled, and the handicapped are his special charges. His children are particularly susceptible to the addictive properties of alcohol. It's better, really, if they don't drink at all.

Among the orishas, Obatala is chief, the king of the white cloth. He is pure, patient, wise, and in many of his aspects, very old. He is magically resourceful and—like the chameleon, who is one of his messengers—able to change his appearance easily. Obatala's head is high and cool. He prevails more by wit, by gravitas, than by force.

His stomach is easily upset, and he prefers bland foods, pale in color, as his offerings—meringues, bread pudding, eggs, white cornmeal. He is a gender-shifter; as many of his roads are female as are male.

To know these things about Obatala is not to know Obatala.

Schuyler found him mysterious and hard to reach.

Ian took confidence and pride from being the son of the king.

For me, Obatala is the filler of the hole at the apex of my ribcage, a hollow that has been there as long as I can remember. I don't know the precise physiology of self-loathing, but whatever acids it releases were neutralized as I came under the protection of Obatala's white cloth, and for the first time, I began to feel at home on the planet and in my own skin. The altar we made for him, with its white linen, its white elephants, its white candles, is a refuge when the senses are weary or confused. When I ring his silver bell and ask for favors, they are granted more often than not.

When Obatala rides his priests, they become ancient and joyous and gentle, tireless in cleansing and embracing the people.

My husband, my son, myself. Obatala picked us up and dusted us off. He smiled upon us. He showed us what a good father could be.

Ritual time is not the world's time. It expands and contracts depending on whether it is empty or full. There is always waiting—so much waiting that you think you will explode, and then more waiting. When something finally happens it is so abrupt, so intense, so unexpected that it doesn't *take* time so much as it *becomes* time, as if the measure of the intervals of our existence then were not the march of imaginary minutes but prayers, divinations, metamorphoses, miracles. Of the waiting, we say, I sat for a long time with nothing to do. I was bored. Of the ritual itself, we say afterward, I wept. I trembled. I was changed.

Maria and Rosi told me I could sleep on their couch the night I received my elekes. That meant I got to stay on after everyone else went home, everyone but Bashezo, a young priest who lived nearby and was in training of some kind, part of the inner circle. The three women sprawled on the couch. I sat a little apart, on a footstool. They plunged into a discussion of a situation they knew well and found troublesome. I felt the urgency without knowing any of the backstory.

From what I could tell, Maria had to make a difficult decision. Rosi gave her supernatural advice. Bashezo gave her real-world tactical advice. Maria listened to them both. Then Rosi stood up. "How about some music?" She danced to the stereo, a sexy salsa step, and put on a CD from Brazil. When the music started playing, it was as if the room itself relaxed a little. Rosi headed back for the sofa, hips moving, center of gravity of low. She danced up to Maria, and for a moment, Maria laid her head against Rosi's belly, and Rosi cradled it there. Then they talked for a while longer about the business of the house, making no effort to include me, but not editing their conversation because I happened to be there, either until Bashezo called it a night. The madrinas gave me a blanket and told me to make myself at home. They turned off the music and the lights and retreated to their room.

The couch was in the very center of the living room. I folded one of the throw pillows under my neck and lay back. The ceiling was streaked with light from the streetlamps outside. I was exhausted by the day's activities, but instead of sleep, what came upon me was a silvery current of energy that made me feel at least as alert as I was tired. I could hear shouts in the distance, and the gunning of engines, and voices speaking softly. Music. The barking of dogs. It seemed as if I could hear the air around me, too, those charged atomic particles pressing on my eardrums. All of Maria's ocha, all of Rosi's, were in that room, encircling me. I imagined I could feel their living presence. For that one night, the couch in the center of the living room was the raft in the center of the sea of life. I was content to float upon it.

Near dawn, just as the first birds were beginning to sing outside, I slept for a couple of hours. At seven I woke up, knowing I had slept enough, collected my things, and left the house quietly, without waking the madrinas. It was their day off, Monday, and I figured they deserved their privacy.

That afternoon, when I stepped off the airplane in Seattle, I scanned the faces waiting at the gate, searching for Schuyler's. It was there, but not entirely familiar. In my absence, anticipating my return, he had shaved off the moustache that had shielded his upper lip for thirty years. He was the same, and not. His eyes lighted up when he recognized me among the travelers, and I had the sensation, seeing him, that I was looking in a mirror.

43

in the neighborhood

Morning is so bright and beautiful I decide to walk to work, by the longest route I can devise. I'm still dressed all in white in the wake of my initiation. Whiteness seems more than sartorial, as if I've become a reflective body, made luminous by the light that falls upon me. My facial muscles default to smiling. There are shadows, of course. There will always be shadows. My daughter is lonely in LA. One of our clients is a jerk. In the week I was gone, my mother developed another bladder infection. I imagine the bacteria that cause these infections survive by eating light. My mother is back in her dark place again.

Somehow this day, with these elekes around my neck, I am able to see what is sad and dark without becoming it. The sun is still warm on my skin. Walking is still a rhythm instrument. My heart feels light inside me. This is new, that others' unhappiness does not require my own. When I reach the four corners with its little grove of alders, I ask Eleggua to open the road for me, then turn left onto the long uphill rise to Madison, the grade just steep enough to make the walk aerobic exercise. Waves of shadow roll across the field of long grass beside the road—that's what I think at first, until I realize the color shifts are made by wind, turning the blades in broad swathes to expose their lighter undersides. A pheasant struts out of the underbrush. Now and then, cars whiz past me, leaving wakes of wind. Then, having given no thought to distance traveled, I arrive at the next and bigger crossroads, at the top of the slope.

There, on my left, is a brand-new apartment building. The sign-board on the sidewalk says WYATT HOUSE ASSISTED LIVING NOW SHOWING. The structure seems to have sprung up from the ground fully formed. It worries me, to have been oblivious to the construction phase, especially of something that turned out to be so big. In any case, it's there now, now showing. I go inside to see what I can see.

Ten days later, we move my mother in.

Scootie the nurse is a gray-haired preppie with a low-riding ponytail, an almond-shaped face, eyebrows magnetically drawn to one another by the thought of something left undone. Sometimes she affixes a gold circle pin to the collar of a white blouse, a sight that transports me straight back to junior high dances and makes me see Scootie as an anachronism, a flower plucked out of one garden of time and trans-planted, only slightly the worse for wear, to another. My daughter, it turns out, ran cross-country at the high school with Scootie's son. Her own mother has been in the island's other assisted living compound almost since the day it opened. The two facilities share owners, and Scootie is the nurse of record for both, scurrying back and forth across the scant crow's-flight mile that lies between them. She is earnest and compassionate and always doing at least two things at once.

After my mother has lived at Wyatt House for two days, Scootie calls me into her office.

"What's in the bag?" she asks.

It's a Rite Aid bag. The answer is, toiletries, paper products, soap. "The basics," I say.

"Pantyhose?"

"Ten pairs."

"Please take them back," Scootie says.

"My mother asked for them in particular."

"Your mother pees right through them," Scootie says.

"So that's why . . ."

"She smells."

"I get it." Finally, I get it.

"It's not uncommon. But she has to switch to knee-highs right away." Scootie grins. "Confiscate the hose she already has. Once she stops wearing them, we can work on diaper-training, too."

Before I go upstairs to visit my mother, I head back to Rite Aid. When I return, I have a couple of six-packs of one-size-fits-all sheer knee-highs in medium taupe. In my mother's apartment, I unpack my plastic sack, item by item.

"Here's your new soap. Here's your new deodorant. Here's your Kleenex. Here's a new lipstick. Here's your pantyhose."

"Those aren't the right kind," my mother says. "You wear that kind with pants, not with skirts."

"The doctor thinks your panty hose have been causing your bladder infections, Mom. He wants you to switch." By now, I know when it's time to invoke The Doctor.

"What's this about a bladder infection?"

"You've had two in a row. You hate them."

"I suppose I do," my mother says.

"So, there's time for a shower before dinner. What do you say?"

"I say phooey. I don't need a shower."

"Actually, Mom, you do."

"I don't *want* one."

"I'll put on the shower music. You take your clothes off."

My mother resists until she hears Frank Sinatra start to sing. She slips out of her skirt and blouse. My mother has her first shower in her new apartment, not a moment too soon. She's lived there two days, and already this room has begun to smell like her old one. Afterward, when she's clean and lotioned and mostly dressed, we experiment with the knee-highs and with the Depends. She assures me that she understands where to find these and how to put them on and where to dispose of them. We conclude that the bottom of her skirt hides the top of her knee-highs, and with no full-length mirror in sight to offer evidence to the contrary, it's almost true. I tell my mother how pretty she looks. She seems at ease and pleased to be clean. "Just in time for dinner," I say.

"Oh, I don't want to go to dinner," my mother says.

"Sure you do. I'll walk you down."

"No, Joyce. I don't think so."

"Here's your purse. Let's hold hands."

My mother takes my hand. The corridor seems impossibly long. No sign marks the turn into the elevator alcove. My mother's apartment is on the third floor and there are no attendants here, not another living soul in sight. While we wait for the elevator to come, we talk about the picture on the wall, a young girl in a white dress reclining on a grassy slope. "I like that," my mother says.

She doesn't like the dining room. The tables, big and round, accommodate six diners, but there are no assigned places, and my mother doesn't know a soul. For a moment, looking at the half-full tables, at the empty ones, I share her anxiety. Two of the tables seem fixed, socially stable. Husbands and wives. We won't try those. Instead, I pick a table where two diners occupy opposing arcs and sit us down between them. "Mind if we join you?" The old man has a hearing aid and a bolo tie. The woman, tiny and bespectacled, says, "Please do," even though we already have. Under the table, I squeeze my mother's hand. A waitress appears with icewater and choices.

I don't eat, just act as hostess, drawing out my companions. None of them initiates, but everyone is willing to respond. The man is a retired accountant. The tiny woman has a daughter who sells real estate. They're genuinely interested to learn that my mother is a lawyer. Our group looks so lively that the remaining seats soon fill up. A dentist in a wheelchair. In a bright green dress with food stains on the chest, a brash old girl whose grasp of ordinary reality seems even less firm than my mom's. I do my best to stir up conversation.

When the waitress brings dessert, I tell my mother I have to go home and make dinner. "It was a pleasure meeting you all," I say, rising before my mother has a chance to protest. At the door of the dining room, when I turn to wave, I see fondness and desolation in the look my mother turns upon me.

The *other* senior facility, the Madison Avenue Retirement Community down by the harbor, is filled with longtime island-dwellers, couples who owned small businesses or taught school, raised families here. Most of the widows and widowers among them still had spouses when they moved in, and in their bereavement, simply continue to be part of a community of old friends. Scootie and her bosses expected the new complex, Wyatt House, to be more of the same. It's not.

Except for a few local couples who got tired of waiting for someone at the MARC to drop dead and make room for them, the residents of Wyatt House are not volunteers. They are not island-dwellers, but the parents of middle-aged children who live on the island. They are not people who planned for their twilight years, but ones surprised to be overtaken by the indignities of old age. They are here because their children moved them here, from New York, from Florida and Michigan and Pennsylvania. For the first time, my mother is truly among her peers, lifelong professionals at the nether end of life. They are oddly lacking in social skills.

"I never would have expected it," Scootie says, "but I guess it makes sense." We're sitting in her office, backroom sociologists swapping anecdotal evidence. I'm pleased to have found somebody who actually thinks about things. She seems to be glad to share what she knows. "The old doctors are the worst. They're used to walking into a room and being treated like God himself. Now that they're feeble or incontinent, they'd just as soon not leave their rooms."

"It's hard to be pompous when you're trailing an oxygen tank."

"Old age was supposed to be for people without advanced degrees," Scootie says. "They take no comfort from being in the same boat with everybody else."

"It's better for my mom now that her memory's shot," I say. "For ten years before it went, as it was going, she was really depressed."

"Old Dr. Q," Scootie says, "is really depressed. His mind's fine but his body's giving out."

Old Dr. Q operated on my best friend's crossed eyes when we were little kids. Forty-five years ago, he was the finest eye surgeon in Seattle. The other night at dinner, he told me how much he hadn't wanted to move to Bainbridge. How much he wished he had the strength to kill himself. He asked me if I wouldn't like to help. I treated it as a joke, although it may not have been.

"What people want is an upscale nursing home." Scootie sighs. "The owners didn't have a clue."

Which brings us full circle back to the subject we started out with, the chronic shortage of trained staff. The owners planned to hire high school kids at minimum wage to vacuum and dust and wait tables in the dining room. Turns out about seventy percent of the residents need help with their medications. At least half could do with some assistance getting dressed and bathing. A significant minority, like my mother, are in reasonably good health physically but demented, the markers *why, when, where* gone missing. I'm here in the office to arrange for escort service for her, to and from meals.

Scootie consults her list, ticking off names. "We can start on three and work our way down, collecting. What I need here is a shepherd."

Our conversation ends there, prematurely, because the receptionist comes in to report that Doc has stolen the Rolodex again.

Even in the midsummer heat, Doc wears a heavy wool suit with wingtips, and his suits smell just like my mother used to, only worse. All day long, caged and kingly, he paces the little lobby. It is far too small to contain his fearsome energy. Doc's energy is fearsome not because it's dark or negative, but simply because there is so much of it. Now it's all directed at the front door. Doc is waiting for his son to come. In the meantime, he appoints himself doorman. Courtly and aggressive, he flirts with women he finds intriguing, or simply follows them to their destination, smiling his swarthy cherub smile. Though his body language is eloquent, he's not much of a talker. Whatever precipitated his dementia has left him between languages, his native Turkish marbled through the English he mastered later on. When the receptionist leaves her post for a moment, he filches things—the Rolodex, the answering machine, the stapler. These are power objects, and Doc is used to having power. Management learns to lock the office at night. Scootie secures the medicine cabinet. By the end of Doc's first week, the receptionist is threatening to quit, and the family is persuaded to adjust Doc's meds. This done, he is less a lion, more a Cheshire cat.

Doc doesn't abandon his vigil, but now, instead of pacing, he sits. Instead of a hurricane, dispersing energy, he becomes a lodestone with a big smile and a smelly suit. The little flock of the demented, those folks who need help finding their way about, collect around him in the lobby. As long as they're well behaved, the receptionist doesn't mind if they hang out. Although at first she doesn't say much, my mother soon becomes part of this company. From after breakfast until dinnertime, there is always a little knot of elders in the lobby, waiting for their children to arrive.

Somehow my mother always knows I'm coming. By the time I step into the canopied walkway in front of the building, she's on her feet and heading for the door. The look of crazed happiness on her face when I turn up reminds me of when my children were small and I was for a time the center of their universe. It is not a feeling I had expected to know again.

44

the reunion

Because relatives from "the old country" have come to visit, the extended family gathers for a picnic at the beach. It's been a long time since anybody but my cousin Orky and her husband has seen my mother. It's been a long time since my mother has seen her brother Ted. There was a space of years, too long, when my mother refused invitations, but dementia has made her game for anything, even going to the beach, with its bittersweet memories of her sister Olga and her brother Emmett, her darker memories of my father and his booze. Because it's breezy by the water, I've bundled her up in my claret-colored parka. With her white curls and her thin legs, my mother looks like Little Red Riding Hood trapped in a time warp. The family buzzes at the sight of her when she emerges from the car. They crowd around to greet her, to check her out. Rather than knowing these people, Anne knows she knew these people, and that's enough. She is gracious to everyone. I stay at her elbow and slowly steer her toward my Uncle Ted.

Ted's sitting in a lawn chair on the corner of the deck, wearing a thick sweater and a benign expression, with something of the prairie dog look my mother's family takes on in age. Although he's deep in his nineties, he recognizes his little sister and at the sight of her rises unsteadily to his feet. Seeing him, my mother walks a little quicker. I help her climb the two stairs to the deck, then they are face-to-face, trembling slightly, my mom's throaty voice and her brother's reedy one saying hello. Ted takes my mother's hand. They make small talk for a while, discussing the seabreeze, the tentative sunshine, and one another's health. As they talk, the family forms a circle, loose and curious, around them, and I can feel their awareness of what's taking place, this meeting of siblings, last survivors of a generation.

My mother suffers her hand to be held, although she doesn't look quite comfortable, and while she's outwardly friendly, a certain reserve in her voice makes me wonder if she really knows who it is she's talking to. Finally, coquettish in the asking, straightforward about not knowing, she asks point-blank, "Who are you?"

He giggles. "Why, I'm your big brother. I'm Ted."

My mother gasps. "What happened to your hair?"

Ted runs a gnarled brown hand over his naked pate. "I haven't had much for the last forty years or so."

"The last time I saw you, you had a full head of hair. Now you're bald as a billiard ball. No wonder I didn't recognize you," my mother says.

My Uncle Ted smiles at this evidence of my mother's addled pate. She chuckles at his baldness. My cousin Shari and I seat them side-by-side in the mild, fresh wind. We wrap their legs in blankets and bring them mugs of hot coffee and a plate of butter cookies to share. A flush of excitement sits on both sets of cheeks just the same way, heightening the resemblance between them. They talk for hours. My mother says the same five things again and again, but Ted doesn't seem to mind. Shari tells me that at home, he'll sit for days and scarcely say a word. The visit lasts until the sun is down and all my mother's bubbles have gone flat from exhaustion.

"I can't believe I didn't recognize my own brother. He's bald as a billiard ball." On the way home, the story of the reunion is already taking shape. For several days my mother remembers, telling it verbatim to anyone who'll listen.

45

spirit work

A number of my friends, all Pisces women, see colored auras around other human beings. This is so naturally part of their perception that they grew up assuming everyone else could see auras, too. Our therapist has her Ph.D. in counseling, but what really makes her good is her gift of seeing, which extends both to how people hold emotion and experience in their bodies and to the spirits that surround them. I envy the eloquent dreamers, my husband among them, whose night visions are full of prophecy or revelation. My son told me recently that he often sees fields of energy around people, as distinctive as fingerprints, tightly knit, of uniform thickness and integrity, or far-flung, ecstatic or erratic, with spikes and sparks, and this seeing is part of how he knows another person. The best diviners I know, whether they use cards or shells, mediate brilliantly between the oracle and the individual. Then there are the mediums, people so available, so spiritually transparent, that other beings borrow their voices to deliver messages. Of those I have known only a few.

My own ways are different from these. If I can keep myself open, things come to me that I need to know. I know that the voices delivering this information do not arise with me; I can distinguish them from my own voice, even though they speak inside my head. The most mystical of my experience is sited in the natural world and uses its creatures as props and vehicles. I don't fully understand how my stories come to me, or what happens to them after they enter the world. My intuition is very strong but does not seem *other*. One night on a beach in Florida, a great blue heron spent the better part of an hour trying to teach me how to fly. Occasionally the dead reach out to me.

Most of us, if we do not deny the testimony of our senses, have ways of understanding the world that resist measurement and transcend easy explanation. Some few are so unconstrained by disbelief that they are able to develop and direct their powers. I long to experience the world as they do.

At Wyatt House, my mother's apartment is on the quiet side of the building and looks down on a large open lot full of grass and trees old enough to be tall, with gnarled trunks and sweeping canopies of leaves. We picked this room above the rest for its bucolic view and the soft green light that on a summer evening shimmers up from the mature orchard below. We thought my mother would be pleased.

During the day, she doesn't mind having the blinds open, but when the light softens and the shadows lengthen a little, when the greens mute down toward dusk, my mother sees things in the orchard that unsettle her. We stand side by side at her window, looking down, and she tries to point them out to me, but I cannot see what she does, no matter how hard I try.

The garage of the house in Oakland has by Maria's labor been transformed into a ritual space. The ceiling is vaulted now, the walls Sheetrocked, the floor covered with linoleum. Two smaller rooms have been added off the main one. The white table is set up against one white wall. Rosi sits on one side of it, Chango Lade, a handsome black woman in her thirties, to the other with her notebook, ready to translate and record the proceedings. My son and I sit side by side, facing the table. I have brought him because we share ancestors as much as genes, because I want him to witness, to be a second set of eyes and ears and insights. When I received my elekes, Maria told me I should have a misa—a guided consultation with ancestral spirits—as soon as possible. Five weeks later, on an August night, I light the candles I have brought with me, while Rosi and Chango Lade pray.

During the invocation, they clap their hands over the altar to drive away unwelcome spirits. When they invite me to approach the table with its clear bowl of water and flickering lights, I clap my hands, too, then learn that I was not supposed to—I've sent a mixed message to the spirits we just summoned. Rather than starting over, Rosi says never mind; we'll move ahead. Doing the wrong thing, right at the beginning, makes me anxious.

Things happen quickly after that. Rosi tells me two infants are attached to me. Have I lost children or aborted them? Once at eighteen, once at thirty-eight, I terminated pregnancies. Once I was too young. Once I was a single mother with two children and didn't feel that my love or money could stretch to a third. Rosi's blunt inquiry requires that I revisit those hard times. My living children know nothing of this. My son sits beside me. The truth is simple, one syllable. Yes. I am willing to tell the truth, but feel a great need to explain myself. Yes, *but*. Chango Lade shakes her head. "Just listen," she says.

Rosi tells me I need to go to a church, light candles, and pray for the spirits of those babies. That way they will be released. Rosi says I lost a third child, as well, perhaps by spontaneous abortion, and the spirit of this child was born with Ian, so that he has two souls.

And then my mother's spirit comes. My mother's spirit does not have Alzheimer's. She is lucid. She makes requests and gives instructions for the care of her impaired self. She tells me a few big, hard-to-swallow facts. I was conceived because my father raped her. Her depression after his death was not mourning but guilt for being relieved at his passing. Her own father was a cruel man.

Then her two sisters speak. When my mother was a child, one of them was kind to her and one was mean. One of them insists now that my mother owes her a huge debt. They will not tell Rosi their names.

Having met a small and surly cavalcade of my ancestors, Rosi tells me that I should take all the family pictures off my boveda. I come from troubled people, and they need more help than I can give them right now.

My mother says she is tired, and departs.

Are there other spirits present who wish to speak?

Until now, Rosi has been Rosi, conveying messages, but suddenly she is no longer Rosi. Her shoulders hunch deeply and her body seems to shrink. Her head sits differently upon her shoulders, so she resembles an aged vulture. Rosi herself is Puerto Rican. Her first language is Spanish. Her English is good but not native. The old man voice that speaks through her now speaks English awkwardly and with an accent that is not Spanish. He tells me many things, including how to set up my boveda in the absence of ancestors. Three brown female spirits will help me, he says. I am to call them Faith, Hope, and Charity. I am to put a glass of water for each one on my table. I am to find a statue of an Indio and put it on my boveda. I am to light candles and spend time with these spirits every day. If I put in the effort, they will teach me how to live.

Chango Lade asks the old man if he has a name. He coughs or chuckles, I can't tell which, and says that we can call him Joe. Chango Lade offers him a cigar, and Joe accepts. The first inhalation nearly chokes him, but after that, he relishes his smoke. He tells me I don't need to feel responsible for so much. I don't have to save the world. I do need to love it. I should spend time with trees. I need to worry less and laugh more. The three brown female spirits will show me what it is to be happy and teach me other things I've never really known.

The session is long. When Rosi comes back to herself, she gives me detailed instructions for the spiritual baths I am to give my mother, the prayers I'm to say on her behalf. They will "cool" her and help to lift up her spirit and clear her head. She tells me to get all artifacts of my father out of my mother's room. Other small rituals, too, she instructs me to do.

When the misa is over, we all go into the house, where Maria and Bashezo are creating an altar for Ochun. Rosi asks us what happened when she was in trance. Chango Lade tells her about Joe. "What language did he speak?" Rosi asks.

"English, but like he didn't really know it very well."

Rosi crows. She wants us to tell her what Joe was like, and what he had to say. After so much hard work, she is giddy and relaxed, happy to have added a new spirit to her collection of familiars.

When we leave the house, my son and I are ravenously hungry. Finally, we find a Jack in the Box that's open and get in line for the drive-thru, twelve cars back. When our cheeseburgers emerge from the window and hour later, we're almost too exhausted to unwrap them. Spirit work exaggerates all appetites.

the magic bath (Anne's turn)

When she is here
They keep their distance
My voice works
I can say things besides
No
Besides
Go away
The singer sings and so
I must take off my clothes
Even though I hate
To be naked
Water is a cat's rough tongue

Licking my raw nerves
And I am afraid if they
See me without my clothes
They will think
I am fair game
She has been gone
A long time
Now the water comes
She has a purple pitcher
She has a white cloth
I cringe
Don't touch me!
But then the sun comes out
Light passes through the water
And turns into summer wind
Sweet on my skin
And even though I cannot smell
I can smell cinnamon
Nothing hurts
Anywhere
And I am not afraid
Even though I am old
I am beautiful
Even though it is short
Life is good
I believe it is love
In the purple pitcher
I believe it is love
In my mind
Even though I ask her nicely
She says she cannot feel
This silver wind

corroboration

Scootie hailed me across the parking lot. "Wait! I want to talk to you."

I waited. I was always dreading the day she'd tell me my mother required more care than Wyatt House was able to provide. Was this it?

Scootie's ponytail bounced as she covered the distance between us. "I'm so glad I caught you." She touched my arm. "I want to know how you changed Anne's meds."

"But I . . ." The next word was supposed to be *didn't.*

"Because the change is just remarkable," Scootie said.

"Well, I . . ."

"If I knew what had made such a difference for Anne, I could suggest it to some of the other families."

"It's not her meds, Scootie."

"Well, something's changed. Her mind is clearer. She's more sociable. It's like she's a new woman."

"That's what *she* said."

"Tell me your secret," Scootie said.

I looked at the gold cross on the gold chain, nestled inside the collar of her white blouse, and chose my words with care. "I did some spiritual work with her," I said. "You know, like praying."

Scootie smiled brightly. "Well, then, I guess it's a miracle."

I didn't disagree.

the leaf

In the Northwest, Labor Day is a watershed. No matter how bright the sun shines, a touch of autumn sobers the air. The very first leaves, still green, drift down from the trees. The heady scent of ripe blackberries turns subtly to the must of fruit past prime. *Memento mori.* The first week of September whispers its prediction that the world must die again. It's a good time for a run.

Ever since I got my elekes in June, I have been a stronger runner. Now, in the wake of the misa, I experiment with running-mantras that include my spirit guides. *Faith, Hope, and Charity, good spirits run with me.* Anything that finesses the mind's tendency to undermine the body is useful, and I like the idea that something so sweaty and down to earth can be a form of prayer. Every run begins with junk thoughts—details, regrets, and resentments. Only after this phase has run its course can new thoughts come. A good mantra courts the empty mind. *Run with me.*

I'm about three, three and a half miles out along the harbor road, and the yammering has pretty much stopped. Not much traffic at midmorning. Not much mother on my mind. The road here is flanked by an encroachment of forest, the deciduous trees still full and green in leaf. Every so often, one leaf lets go and dizzies down. Every leaf that falls is a little needle of poignancy, pricking my meditation. I watch. I feel. I like the feeling.

I round a long curve where metal railings buttress the shoulders of the road. High above me, a leaf lets go. Another. I watch how gently, how lazily they fall. A third casts off and I watch it, too. Instead of falling down directly, this leaf finds itself a little breeze. It buoys up so gallantly it makes me smile. There. It's headed down again. The leaf has my attention now. I want to see its landing on the road.

Ten or twelve feet up, the leaf curtails its descent the ways seagulls do sometimes, planes out laterally for half a dozen yards. I expect it to drop, but it rallies, bouncing up again. How odd. How amusing. I stop running to watch the show. Once I do, the show changes, no longer a matter of mere up and down, but a dance with long trills of sideways motion, with swoops and swirls and whirlwinds, giddy little pirouettes described on air. I watch because the dance is beautiful. I watch because it is impossible. Every instant, I expect it will end.

It doesn't end. Instead, the dance grows more extravagant, the dips lower and more dangerous, the leaps swifter and higher, more masterful. It is such a small thing, a leaf refusing to fall, a leaf dancing in defiance of gravity, but the longer it dances, the more enchanting it is. Around it, other leaves cast off and in short order fall to earth. A car, two cars appear and pass by, creating an airstream that makes the leaf take flight, up, up, and then sink down. Each time, I think the dance must end, but even when the air grows still, the leaf continues to dance above the road. It dances so sinuously, so flirtatiously, for so *long,* that I begin almost reluctantly to understand that at this moment one or several of the laws of nature have been repealed. I am sure that thinking this will end the dance.

My neck grows stiff from looking up. Without taking my eyes from the leaf, I move to the shoulder of the road and sit down on the metal barricade. The dance is stately now, and graceful, a minuet. Suddenly I understand that it is not the leaf dancing but the wind. The leaf is making visible the dance of wind. My heart beats faster. Suddenly, necessarily, I am in awe of the wind.

Part of me wants to deny the testimony of my senses. Part of me wants to leap toward meaning. I outwait any possibility of fluke. Ten minutes later, when I turn toward home, the leaf is still aloft.

47

my mother, lost and found

For eight or ten weeks in the late summer and early fall of 1999, my mother is healthy and happy and wholly available to me. She lives so close now that our adventures can be spur of the moment and mundane. We go to the grocery store together, to the post office and to the bank. We go out for coffee in the afternoon. I bring her to our house for lunch or dinner or simply to hang out and play with the dog. We go for drives in the sunshine, to see how the leaves turn color, to watch the full moon rise. If my daughter, home from college, is working at the restaurant on the waterfront, we can sit at one of her tables on the deck, visit with her, and leave a great big tip.

In midsummer, Schuyler inherits a plot in the local P-patch. Suddenly he is a master gardener again, skilled and determined. We double-dig with compost, fertilize, sprout seeds and plant them. When we go to water late on summer afternoons and no one else is around, I find myself singing to the garden, holding long wordless vibrato notes somewhere in the alto range as I stride around the perimeter. Schuyler digs up a perfect lingam and places it upright in the very heart of the plot. Fast and hardy, choys first, then lettuces and chards, our garden grows. Around it, rototilled plots yield scraggly cornstalks, retarded lettuces, assorted weeds. Our garden becomes locally famous for its abundance. It produces far more than we can possibly eat, so we bring boxes full of greens to the cook at Wyatt House. He's glad to have them, and Schuyler is pleased to feed the elders from his soil. Even though my mother usually shoves vegetables to the side of her plate and leaves them there, we figure some of our produce makes its way into her diet.

My mother is eighty-seven and mentally diminished, I am fifty-one years old, but for a little while, we have the relationship I always dreamed of. Our lives entwine. We are utterly attentive to one another. Everywhere we go, my mother holds my hand. Every time we join hands in our travels, she says, "And a little child shall lead them." Sometimes she says, "Who would have thought?" One day in the Safeway parking lot, I ask her, "Thought what?"

"That we would ever be like this," my mother says.

Some days my mother says her apartment reminds her of her college days. Sometimes she thinks she's *in* college. More than once, she tells me she'd like to get a job. In a way, she has one.

There are four tables in my mother's apartment—a kitchen table, a coffee table in front of the loveseat, an orange end table by her big chair, a nightstand beside her bed. I make sure that all four are covered with artifacts to spark remembrance—photo albums and scrapbooks, boxes of loose snapshots, camphor chests full of cards and letters, stories my mother wrote in college, books of poetry she loved when I was little—not all at once but in controlled doses, to prevent undue clutter of space or brain. When she's alone in her apartment, she dives into her past. When I come to visit in the evening, she often shares what she's found.

Sometimes she reads poems to me, standing very straight at one end of her little living room, holding the book in both hands, as she must have done in her college speech classes. If she were reading a story from *Newsweek* now, she would stumble over words and struggle with syntax, but somehow, she can deliver poetry with clarity and conviction. I am the easiest of audiences, always willing to laugh out loud at "The Cremation of Sam McGee" or ante up a tear over James Whitcomb Reilly's maudlin verses. When my mother is done, I clap. She blushes and bows.

One day, in one of the carved Chinese chests that were a gift from grateful clients, my mother finds a packet of letters my father wrote her the year before they married, when he was on a cross-country car trip with his mother, father, and younger sister. She reads them carefully, savoring deft descriptions of family behavior, his compliments and accounts of missing her. They're creditable love letters, and make it possible for me to imagine a time before acrimony and alcohol, when my parents were in love. Because of the holes in her short-term memory, the best phrases give my mother pleasure again and again. Over and over, she reads them aloud. Each time, I pretend the words are new to me.

"That's really something, isn't it?" My mother sighs and lets her favorite of the letters rest on her lap. "I wonder whatever happened to him, anyway."

"He died in 1988."

"Did he?" my mother says. "Did he ever marry, do you know?"

"He married you."

My mother laughs. "Oh no. I never married. Never had children. I never wanted to, you know."

"Then who am I?"

My mother cocks her head and looks at me closely, a little smile playing on her lips. "I don't really know," she says.

One night after dinner, I let myself get drawn into life at home. Maybe my son wanted me to listen to a couple of songs from a new Ani DiFranco album, or help him work on an audition monologue. Maybe my husband and I fell into a conversation. I can't remember now. Night fell, and I still hadn't made my way to Wyatt House. I'd already decided it would be a quick trip. No shower, just into the PJs and a goodnight kiss. Then the phone rang. It was the night attendant.

"Oh my god, look at the time," I said, guilty. "I'll be right there."

"Does that mean your mother's not with you?"

"No, she's not here. I'm on my way there."

The night attendant was brand-new. I believe it was her second night on duty. Even though there were maybe forty people living in the building, there was only one of her. After a long silence, she said, "I hate to say this, but I think we've lost your mother."

All the lights are on. The bathroom door is closed. Not knowing what I expect, I open it. The bathroom is empty. My mother's apartment is empty. The night attendant keeps telling us how sorry she is. Schuyler and I question her calmly. When did she last see Anne? Where was she? Whom was she with? The night attendant has only the vaguest recollection of events after dinner. Mrs. P had an "episode." When that had been dealt with, it was time to pass out the evening meds. When she got to my mother's apartment with my mother's meds, my mother wasn't there.

We divide the building into thirds, Schuyler, the night attendant, and I. Starting with the first floor, she'll knock on all the residents' doors. We'll comb the rest of the building, the empty units. I try to beam in on my mother—*Where are you?*—but the silence of Wyatt House at night is imperturbable. I check the offices and the laundry room, the game room, the beauty parlor, the library. If my mother is any of these places, she is not happy. She is not well. People have been calling her name for forty-five minutes now. I find myself looking behind furniture, at the floor. Schuyler goes into the dining room, the pantry, the dark kitchen, the walk-in freezer. When all the rooms have been visited, Schuyler and I go outside, into the chilly autumn night. I walk around the building, prodding bushes. He takes the parking lot, then drives around the block. When all of this fails to produce my mother, we call the police.

Two policemen arrive, exuding self-assurance. If my mother has not been found, we've not looked properly. Step by step, they replicate our search, with no better results. The night attendant is beside herself by now. In the pit of my stomach, I despair of a good outcome. Dumbly, we follow the officers as they open and close doors. After all three floors have been scoured for the second time, we return to the lobby. After the older of the policemen comes out of the public bathroom, he turns to the door beside it. Tries the knob. Locked.

"What's this?" he says.

"Oh, that," the night attendant says. "That's the Furnished Model Unit."

"Open it up, please," says the cop.

But the night attendant can't open it up. It is the one door that must remain locked at all times. The marketing director is in Florida. The custodian doesn't answer his phone. One of the policemen says something about shooting the lock, but I think he's kidding. Before they leave, the cops assure me they'll let us know immediately if someone finds my mother wandering the streets. Finally, around eleven o'clock, the marketing director's husband returns the night attendant's call. He agrees to bring us the master key. While we wait, I knock on the locked door of the Furnished Model Unit. I call my mother's name. The fairy tale *Bluebeard,* with its one forbidden room, resides in my mind. By the time we have the master key, I am almost afraid to open the door.

Inside the Furnished Model Unit, all the lights are on. With the silk flowers and the waxed fruit and the scent of roses rising from the bowl of potpourri, the place gives the illusion of being occupied. In the little bedroom in the little single bed with the little yellow-and-baby-blue quilt pulled all the way up beyond her chin, a little old woman is fast asleep. She has squared her shoes neatly beside the bed. The night attendant weeps with relief. Schuyler laughs. I do a little of both.

"I don't understand how she got in here, it's always locked tight," the night attendant says, and, "We might as well let her finish out the night here, she's so peaceful."

It's a kind thought, but I insist on waking my mother up and returning her to her own apartment and putting her in her own bed, in case the Furnished Model Unit is not furnished with plastic sheets.

When my mother wakes up, she has no idea where she is, or how she got here, and I feel as I often have when my kids have gone astray—that lightning turn from anxious love to anger, once the missing turn up safe.

48

the darkness returns

Darkness is the aggregation of mischance. The female night attendant hurts her back and is replaced by a male night attendant. If he so much as touches her arm, my mother curses and strikes out at him. An aneurysm breaks loose in Doc's brain. Mrs. P has a heart attack. Nettie's children move her to a nursing home. One by one, the happy band of demented elders who passed their days together in the Wyatt House lobby diminishes, until only my mother is left. She catches a cold. Scootie asks me to get her a decongestant. The side effect of the decongestant is dehydration. The side effect of dehydration is another bladder infection. My mother loses her appetite and takes to her bed. Malnutrition deepens her confusion.

The rains come. The days grow short. There is a reason ancient people believed the door between October and November was a passage between the worlds of the living and the dead. Darkness presses against the windows of my mother's apartment. It fills her heart.

One night in this time, when her ghosts were particularly troublesome, I sat on the edge of my mother's bed, holding her hand and stroking her hair. Schuyler was there with me. We'd spent an hour or more mostly listening to Anne, murmuring agreement or asking the occasional question to keep the words coming. Her rhetoric and her syntax remained utterly convincing, even as concrete nouns came unstuck from their usual meanings and went into freefall inside her sentences. Perfectly formed and cogent statements went wonky as *carrot* or *rutabaga* took the place of whatever noun she meant to say, so that her speech became a whimsical word salad, punctuated with little pockets of stark and brilliant truth. *The carrot came out of the clouds.* My mother's language gift was so well developed that observing this process, this slow unwinding, was at least as compelling as watching my children acquire their language skills in the first place. It made both Schuyler and me her willing audience.

This night her world was bleak, and her language was vaguer than ever, the generic noun *deal* being seized to stand for whole great chunks of history, affect, and motive. The people behind her pronouns, *he* and *they*, were never identified. It was a tale of treachery nonetheless. A bad deal, a shady deal, a very complicated deal. Rapt and lost, we listened. It was something like trying to watch a movie from the dark side of the screen; my mother could see the past, fully evoked and in exquisite detail, while we were left with the flickering shadows her denatured words cast in our minds. She was quite agitated by the tale, exhausted by the telling.

As it got later, I helped my mother out of her clothes and into her nightgown, eased her from the edge of the bed, where she was holding forth, into the nest of her covers. She stared in utter terror at a fixed point just beyond the foot of her brass bed.

"Mom, what is it? What do you see?"

She shook her head slightly and kept staring. Her face took on undertones of putty and mud. "Mom?"

Again, she shook her head.

"Is there anything I can do to help?"

"I have terrible memories," she said. "Terrible things happened. You don't know."

"I'm willing to listen, Mom."

"I can't tell."

Now Schuyler spoke up. "Talking about the hard things can cut them down to size, Anne. It can help."

"You don't know," my mother said.

"You don't have to carry this alone," Schuyler said.

"We'll keep you safe, Mom," I said.

"You can't."

I stroked her hair. "We love you."

"Terrible things," she said, her gaze unwavering.

I kissed her forehead. "Do you want to sleep with a light on tonight?" I asked her.

"Yes."

"Do you want a glass of water?"

"No."

"Shall I put the TV on low, for company?"

"No."

"Goodnight then, sweetie. I'll see you tomorrow."

"What time?"

"I'm not sure."

It was not until I got up to leave that I understood what she was staring at so hard. It was the formal framed photograph of all eight siblings, the five sons standing shoulder to shoulder in the back row, dressed in somber suits, the three daughters, blonde, redhead, and brunette, seated in the front. Everyone looks quite adult and serious except for my mother, who wears long dark sausage curls and a sweet smile. She is all of thirteen. Her brother Emmett, rear, second from the right, has the shadow of a grin on his lips, a twinkle in his eye. If she is thirteen, he is thirty. The year is 1926. The children are gathered for the funeral of their father.

As soon as I got home that night, I thought better of leaving my mother alone. I grabbed a pillow and a blanket and went back to Wyatt House. My mother did not seem surprised to see me. In the last few years, I had been bringing her stuffed animals—two cats, a chihuahua, a frog, and a bear—to join the donkey, named Alben for Harry Truman's vice president, that she kept on her bed. My mother professed to enjoy their company. That night, after I bedded down on the floor, the animals began to misbehave.

The dog leapt upon the cat. "Hey kitty, let's fuck."

The cat protested. "Leave me alone, dog."

The dog: "I want you now."

The cat: "Go fuck yourself, dog."

My mother held the cat in one hand, the dog in the other. She did both voices. I'm not sure who started it, but the animals had a big, no-holds-barred fight, throwing themselves fiercely against each other and growling without words. When the fight was over, my mother put them back in their corner, turned out her bedside light, and wished me goodnight.

The puppet show amazed me. In fifty years, I'd never heard my mother acknowledge that such a thing as sexual desire existed, much less make play of it. In the darkness, her breathing soon went shallow and abraded into snores. She slept fitfully. Every time she moved, the brass bed creaked a little and the plastic undersheet crinkled. I was tired and uncomfortable and filled with the conviction that I needed to stay awake and keep watch over my mother. I don't know what I expected to happen.

The night was long and airless. I must have drifted into a shallow sleep, because more than once I startled alert when I thought I heard footsteps in the room. I kept my elekes around my neck and said the Lord's Prayer many times inside my head, as a kind of prophylactic against disease and death. A couple of times, my mother rose up into a foggy consciousness. I brought her water and made her sip it. At last, the calls of crow and house finch in the orchard below heralded morning. My mother's breathing deepened and slowed. For a while, I stood beside her bed and watched her sleep. In the dimness, I thought her color was a little bit improved.

I left my mother's apartment thinking I'd make coffee, have a little run, and start my workday early, but by the time I'd traveled the three minutes home, my whole body was stiff and achy. My cheeks were hot. A headache slammed in my right temple and I could hardly walk, much less go running. All my life, I have been relentlessly healthy. The way I felt was unfamiliar and frightened me, something especially nasty coming on. I drank water, took Tylenol, and went to bed.

When I woke up, hours and hours later, I was fine. I called Scootie at Wyatt House to find out how my mother was. Scootie told me she'd slept all day. Less than an hour before, her fever had broken so monumentally that it soaked her nightgown, her sheets, even her blankets. "You wouldn't believe that dry old body could hold so much fluid," Scootie said.

My mother suffered herself and her bed to be cleaned up. She suffered herself to be escorted to the dining room, where she had not gone in several days, but she did not eat her dinner. When we arrived later, to take her back to her room, my mother was standing in the lobby all by herself, motionless, staring out the glass panel of the front door into the night. Her thick white hair was matted from her sojourn in the bed, and everything about her that might have turned up—lips, shoulders, eyebrows—now turned down. The tops of her knee-high pantyhose showed underneath the hem of her black skirt. Her eyes were vacant. We had to come close and speak to her before she knew us. When she talked back, it seemed to be across a big distance. The word *zombie* darted through my mind.

Later that night, I called Rosi in Oakland to see if there was anything more I could do to help my mother. She gave me instructions for a ritual with candles and prayers.

"What should I expect?" I asked her.

"I think it might be your mother's time. This will either make her better or help her go peacefully," Rosi said.

I read all the instructions back to her, to make sure I had them right.

49

emergency room, full moon

Thursday morning, my mother's fever was still down and she was up and about, so when the nurse-practitioner suggested admitting her to the hospital for the weekend for observation, I thought it was safe to wait and see. Friday Scootie told me she hadn't left her room or eaten much all day. Saturday morning found me sitting on the edge of her brass bed, feeding her small bites of a cinnamon roll, interspersed with sips of orange juice. My mother had always loved to flirt with Schuyler, so he sat on the couch, trying to tease her out of her grim mood. As her blood sugar rose a bit, her spirits did, too. We got her out of bed so I could change the sheets. I gave her a spit bath and a clean nightgown. Schuyler rubbed her back while I brushed her hair.

"They're going to bring you up some lunch in a couple of hours. I want you to eat it," I said.

"What's the point?" my mother said.

For a moment, I heard the lawyer in her voice. It was cross-examination, time for the hard questions. I thought of two answers and said them both. "Alex is coming home for Thanksgiving. I love you."

My mother harrumphed. I lifted the water cup to her lips and she drank a little more. I explained that we had to go into the city, to the annual Bookfair, and do a cooking demonstration from Schuyler's new book. "Stir-fried geoduck and baked stuffed oysters," I told her. "Then we're going to come back here and take you to the hospital, okay?"

"What do I have to go to the hospital for?" my mother said.

It was another good question. This time, I simply said, "Because."

• • •

When we got back, at the tail end of the afternoon, my mother lay in her bed in a dark room. The bedding was soaked with urine. Whoever brought her lunch tray had simply left it on the kitchen counter. Anne was hunkered down. Existing. I found myself surfing waves of anger and guilt.

It took a while to get her cleaned up again, and another while to get a little food in her, still a third while to discover that instead of prearranging her admission to the hospital in Bremerton, as we'd requested the doctor on call had left us the cryptic message, "Just take her to the Emergency Room." By the time we actually got there, it was going on eight o'clock, and my mother had rallied miraculously.

It was the night of the full moon. The Harrison Hospital Emergency Room was a human zoo. My mother sat primly in her black lawyer suit and expressed her disdain for the pained and scruffy souls surrounding us, the sliced fingers and broken bones, the heart attacks in progress, the screaming babies with their exhausted mothers. Every time we moved up the list a little, another drag-racing teenager would smash his car, another domestic dispute would turn violent enough to draw blood, another diabetic would go into insulin shock. An aging hippie couple, he in denim bellbottoms, she in fringed leather, long unwashed and junkie thin, wandered from the admitting desk to the public telephone, hoping to score from one source or the other. The aroma they gave off was an archeology of addiction—fresh alcohol the fruity top note on a deep chord of metabolic despair. My mother, to be honest, was less than daisy-fresh herself.

"What are we doing here?" she asked indignantly, every ten minutes or so. After the first hour, I got tired of explaining and just said, "We're waiting."

Three and a half hours later, they moved us into a cubicle. The nurse took my mother's vital signs, which, apart from a scant degree of lingering fever, were just fine. Sometime after midnight, a doctor appeared. He looked at my mother, sitting in a chair. He looked at the vitals. "How are you feeling?" he asked her.

"I feel fine," my mother said.

The doctor looked from her to us. "This is not a hotel you can check your elderly parents into because you want the weekend off," he said.

Schuyler is the calmest, the most patient of men, but his equanimity did not extend this far. "If we wanted the weekend off, we would have left her in Assisted Living." If these words seem mild, imagine them as dry ice.

It took a moment for the testosterone flare to subside. The doctor turned back to my mother and began to inquire about her health history. Item by item, she said no. She said it very convincingly, with great dignity. No cancer. No open-heart surgery. No weight loss. No high blood pressure. No cardiac arrhythmia. No loss of appetite. No incontinence. No bladder infections. No depression. No Alzheimer's disease. Every time I tried to amend my mother's answers, the doctor said, "Don't interrupt the patient." When he had run through his list, he said, "There's nothing wrong with this woman. Not enough to justify admission." He turned and left the room.

I went outside and found the nurse. I explained. I begged. I may have threatened. I nearly cried. "Doctor's a little tense tonight," she said. "It's been awfully busy."

"I understand," I said. "Still, we wouldn't be here if my mother didn't need attention."

"You hold on," the nurse told me. "I'll see what I can do."

It was after two A.M. when I knelt beside my mother's hospital bed to kiss her goodnight.

"You two go on home and get a good night's sleep," the nurse told us as we left.

In the morning, when I called the nurses' station to see how my mother was, the charge nurse told me they were giving her IV fluids.

She'd eaten some Jell-O. Then the nurse's perky, reassuring voice dropped a little, grew confidential. "Your mother doesn't know where she is or why she's here," she said. "She's really deeply confused. Her chart doesn't mention it, but she seems to have almost no short-term memory at all."

"You know, I was aware of that," I said.

50

gentle care

On every issue related to aging, Schuyler's parents have been the antithesis of mine. They've acknowledged the inevitable and planned for it, a process that began with research and ended with considered decisions, made well in advance of extremity. Casa Bernardo, the San Diego senior complex where they've lived for more than ten years now, was under construction when they bought in. In that decade, they've been instrumental in building a strong community, and each of his parents knows it will be there to support whichever of them is left behind. Their financial affairs are so well managed that they may succeed in their half-joking goal of spending their estate down to zero at the moment of their departure from this plane. Schuyler's father, a respected dental educator still active in the field well into his eighties, heads the committee to fashion the community's institutional response to its demented members. It was he who alerted me to the concept of Gentlecare.

A Gentlecare Alzheimer's facility is a fairy tale turned inside out, time standing sidewise, a small, logic-defying miracle in a society wedded to the bottom line. It is a facility designed and operated not for the convenience of the staff, but for the comfort and safety of the residents. It is a bubble blown around a disease, and inside its shimmering borders, one is not wrong to be afflicted, one is not a problem to be managed. One is simply a human being living out a stage of his or her life with dignity, grace, and freedom. The freedom is to live according to the cycles of one's own body clock. To rove the full limits of the kingdom without physical or chemical restraint. To be part of a company of fellow adventurers. To expect kindness and approval and assistance from the small army of benevolent soldiers who oversee the affairs of the court. To feel one's feelings. To honor one's impulses. To accept one's limitations. To be exempt from either stress or shame. The charter of a Gentlecare facility is deeply idealistic and humane. The thing itself, in practice, is a little crazy, a little comical, a little gross and messy. It is infinitely fluid.

Imagine a Montessori boarding school where the lights are on twenty-four hours a day, where the pupils suffer all the sundry afflictions of age, and you'll have at least a shadow of the reality. Gentlecare is imaginative and ambitious and extraordinarily civilized. It is also breathtakingly expensive.

After her hospital stay in Bremerton, my mother was eligible for two weeks of Medicare-paid "rehabilitation," which was, in essence, two weeks in a conventional nursing home, with a little physical therapy thrown in. Messenger House, just ten minutes from my house on Bainbridge, combines nursing-home facilities with two Gentlecare Alzheimer's units, to serve patients at different stages of the disease. During the two-week hiatus, I weighed alternatives.

One was to rent a condo in our complex, hire one or two shifts of nursing care a day, and take up the slack myself. If we had been dealing with a disease that came with a time schedule, this would have been a fine alternative. It would have assured that I could be present and helpful for the whole process of my mother's dying, which I was quite willing to do. At that time, though, it seemed perfectly possible that my mother would live another ten years, which made the cost too high.

The second alternative was to partner with another family who had a parent living at Wyatt House and to split the cost of one or two shifts of private care a day, taking up the slack myself. But I already knew the limitations of the existing Wyatt House staff, and of the environment: even if the care were adequate, the tendency toward social isolation was extreme.

Conventional nursing homes are better suited to people with debilitating physical disorders than to the relatively healthy Alzheimer's patient. Their response to the demented is to make them tractable through sedation. This, too, was a poor choice for my mother.

Then there was Gentlecare. A big, open common room full of natural light by day, soft yellow light at night. An enclosed garden, with plenty of room to sit or walk without getting lost. Dormitory-style living, mostly two to a room, though many residents, we were told, had little proprietary sense of space and tucked up wherever they happened to land. *Mine* and *thine* dissolved into *ours*. Don't be surprised, we were told, to see your mother's dress on someone else. Should your parent commence a sexual liaison with another resident, a not-unheard-of occurrence, we will notify you and seek your permission before allowing the affair to proceed. Understand that arguments between inmates may flare into sudden violence, we were told; it is not entirely impossible that your parent will end up with a black eye or a fat lip. The staff is alert and usually able to break things up before any serious harm is done. To allow freedom is to risk disorder.

When we visited, the first person we saw was Doc, as recovered from his aneurysm as he would ever get and dressed in khakis and flannel shirt, a straw hat hovering like a rattan halo about his round brown face, comfortable in the wingback chair he favored as his own. He was smiling faintly when we walked in, but when we waved to him, Doc's grin deepened until it gave off light.

Five thousand dollars a month, not including the almost five hundred dollars worth of prescription medications my mother consumed each thirty days, all out of pocket until all of her assets were gone. Then Medicaid would kick in to help with the difference between her pension and the expense of keeping her.

It was the feel of the place, finally, that sealed my decision.

It was serene.

51

a Christmas story

In the fall of 1999, as a declaration of independence from the tyranny of voice-obliterating editors, to provide ourselves a forum as writers and activists, Schuyler and I started a website, www.food-ist.com. Some of the content is political, some is practical, some is literary. Some is guest-written by friends. Everything is a food story; that's the tongue-in-cheek, chew-thoroughly-before-you-swallow premise of the endeavor. Its effect, in those months shadowed by my mother's decline, was to give us both a little room to be ourselves. The Foodist, of course—that opinionated, kitchen-smart, world-traveling, cookbook-reviewing wise man in an apron with a prep knife in one hand—is Schuyler. I, as consort of the Foodist, was happy to contribute what I could. Someday, I figured, we could add a coffee house to the site, where disaffected poets and fiction writers would find the same kind of forum we provided for those with something to say about food. That would be my bailiwick. We weren't thinking Public Access, either. We were both quite willing to exercise some quality control.

My mother moved into Gentlecare at Messenger House on Thanksgiving Day. Late one afternoon, three weeks later, Schuyler and I wrote this Christmas story for the Foodist. While the pronoun and the point of view belong to Schuyler, the language and the perceptions came almost equally from both of us. It's the first and only time either of us ever experienced such dissolution of writer's ego into a common voice. Perhaps, in that, it echoes the communal spirit of Gentlecare.

The Baby Cheese Ball

A Christmas Story

Perhaps because they live with a food guy, our sons speak a kind of comestible slang. Since they're inventive lads, "tastes like chicken" quickly transmogrified to "tastes like cheese." Upon entering high school, Ian left cheese behind, but Farrell continues to riff on the theme. "You ate too much cheese for breakfast," he'll sometimes say. What this means, we're not all that certain, except that he says it with great conviction. The most intriguing of his inventions is the cheese monkey. It is something he calls anyone who is out of favor or behaving weirdly or asking him to empty the dishwasher or turn off the television set. Joyce and I are often referred to in this wise.

I mention this only because of the Baby Cheese Ball, whom we might not have recognized at the Messenger House Christmas Party had it not been for a full year of preparation.

I'd filled two paper plates with the delectable offerings of the Messenger House Christmas smorgasbord, one for my mother-in-law, Anne, and the other for Virginia, who happened to be sitting in her wheelchair at the same table. I had complimented Virginia on her nails. She gave me one of those "No duh" looks and explained that she had been a beautician. Those were not plastic nails, neither, she assured me. The real thing, and she had done the painting herself, a bright claret red. She didn't want a thing from the smorgasbord when I offered to fetch it, but when I put her plate in front of her, she said it was the nicest thing any young man had ever done for her. It's not every day I'm called a young man.

I had forgone the pleasure of peeled shrimp. They had that melting-snowcone look about them. Instead, I loaded up on teriyaki drumettes, mini fishcakes, both barbecue and sweet-and-sour little meatballs, and those extremely mini cheese-and-spinach quiches you find frozen at Costco. There was thin-sliced ham and thin-sliced turkey by the platterful, and you could tell the difference because one was pink and the other wasn't. I grabbed sliced mini-bagels from the basket, dolloped a little mustard on each plate, and before I left the buffet, impulsively snagged several individual-sized cheese balls, a seasonal favorite. (Did you know that if you query Yahoo! for "cheese balls" you get 857 responses?)

Anne looked suspiciously, somewhat dismissively at the plate of food I put in front of her, but that's been Anne's default response to most things for some time. "She's being a cheese monkey," Farrell would say. Then Anne tucked right in, struggling with a plastic fork to chip bits of meat off the drumettes. Anne was never one to pick up her chicken with her fingers. Short-term memory may be ephemeral, but attitudes appear to last forever.

Maggie came by to see what Anne was up to, but Anne ignored her. Maggie has a lump on the side of her face about the size of a baseball that she tends to cradle with one hand. She scoots about in a wheelchair and hollers at people in a froggy voice. When families began to gather in the common room at Messenger House to celebrate Christmas with their demented elders, Maggie would throw up her arms at any baby, toddler, or family pet, and bark "How old are you?" Pure delight suffused her ravaged face, the kind of joy you sometimes glimpse on the faces of new mothers when they kiss their babies on the tops of their soft heads.

Virginia wanted to know who in hell let in the children. She was truly shocked. "Folks start drinkin' around here, you know, it's gonna get kinda wild," she assured us. That's when I began to realize the conversation Joyce and I'd been having with Virginia, convincing on the surface, was somewhat provisional in the particulars. She had taken me for a chivalrous barfly. According to her, we were somewhere in Pennsylvania, not on Bainbridge Island in Washington state.

We'd moved Anne, an eighty-seven-year-old retired lawyer, into

Messenger House just three weeks before, on Thanksgiving Day. Her tenancy in the Gentlecare dementia unit was all about facing up to the fact that she needs twenty-four-hour care and twenty-four-hour company, that she's no longer up to even the pretense of independence. Once it had been removed from her, and from us, it was easy to see the enormous stress we had all been carrying as we maintained the fiction that she could dress herself or find her own room or put herself to bed at night. In the absence of that burden, her frail form has fleshed out by twelve pounds, and she giggles like a schoolgirl.

Anne poked with her fork at the remains on her plate. "What's this?" she asked of the lumpen cheese thing. "It's the Baby Cheese Ball," Joyce said. She and I heard the liturgical echo right away. So, apparently, did Virginia. "Son of the Big Cheese," Joyce carried on, "that shiny white wheel of Roquefort you see in the sky." In call as in response I added, "The Father, Son, and Neufchatel."

The Baby Cheese Ball was a big hit, or maybe it was just that Joyce and I were laughing pretty hard that made our companions snicker, too. Then "Silent Night" started playing on the background boombox, and Anne started singing in a high, reedy voice, singing to no one in particular, singing along with that troubled look that says she knows there are high notes somewhere just around the corner, notes she reached for and in her fashion snared—"Slee-eep in heavenly peace." And she made it through the whole song, seeming even more the happy young girl, leaving behind the grief and depression and the mild paranoia of the recent past. Smiling through the high notes. A little bashful. But awfully proud.

As we drove home that night, the Big Wheel of Roquefort in the Sky was just off round.

52

new year's news

At a bembe on the first day of the new millennium, Eleggua, orisha of the crossroads, opener of the way, came down on Rosi. He was puckish and sly and danced with pelvis-thrusting pride in his huge mimed member. Eleggua is like that, no friend of solemnity. After he danced for a while, Eleggua/Rosi jumped up on a counter and sat cross-legged, holding court. Schuyler stood on line to salute him. As soon as he finished, Eleggua motioned for Schuyler to turn around. When he did, Eleggua climbed on his shoulders like a two-year-old at the mall and proceeded to ride Schuyler in and out among the dancers as if he were a particularly supple pony, while his rider snatched the caps off the heads of babalawos and tossed them to the ground. He rode until he found Maria, then told her in Spanish that Schuyler must make his ocha within the next eighteen months. He must become a priest.

It was a long-awaited message, life-changing for my husband. For us all.

As the first crocuses poked up out of the ground, as the days grew longer and lighter, I found myself saying two prayers. I prayed that my mother would live as long as she took pleasure in her life. And I prayed for winds of change to blow through mine, to waft away stagnation and all I did not need.

Toward the end of March I got a call from an old friend, telling me his startup had just received its first round of venture capital funding. The previous fall, I'd donated a Sunday to getting the concept of the business down on paper. Now, retroactively, he wanted to pay me for my time. And of course, he wanted to show off the new Seattle loft offices. My friend's enthusiasm was a good deal more persuasive than his business plan, but it was a heady time, when the improbable seemed inevitable, when other people's money flowed as freely as the champagne at a debutante's wedding, when every smart kid got a chance to play entrepreneur. My friend's idea was that you could play Robin Hood and get rich at the same time by selling legitimate "bootlegs" of live rock concerts over the Internet. After a couple hours' indoctrination, I wanted to play, too.

A week later, I was editorial director, both the oldest employee of the company and its sole female executive. Schuyler signed on as a program manager. Our relative maturity and our stable relationship were supposed to help ground a young corporate culture—kind of a mom-and-pop mandate. We had salaries and benefits and stock options. We bought cell phones and Palm Pilots. We had exciting work to do.

My first assignment was to create a new corporate website and have it on-line in a week. I was so stoked that instead of telling my friend it was impossible, I hired a couple of extraordinary designers with whom I still love working and took a crack at his deadline. Ten days later, we went live with a stylish piece of work that much bigger companies were soon emulating. Schuyler and I subcontracted out our existing commitments and put our little communications company in mothballs for a while.

That after three years of taking care of other people's business we felt free to do so was a gift of Gentlecare.

On the first Sunday, at the end of our very first week of work, I went over to Messenger House to see my mom. I wanted to lay my new treasures at her feet, as children do.

the theatre of sky

Messenger House sits on a high bluff above a beach that faces north and east. A wall's width of tall windows looks out across Puget Sound to an horizon made jagged by the distant peaks of the Cascade range.

That Sunday afternoon, my mother sat by herself in an armchair, facing out. Whether she could make out the ghostly shapes of the far mountains or the little moving specks of freighters in the shipping lanes, I don't know, but there's no doubt she and everything around her were bathed in the soft blue light of early spring. I pulled a chair up close to hers and put my arm around her. That way we were both members of the audience in the theatre of sky.

I was full of my new job, a busy little squirrel with many nuts of news, but my mama was not hungry for nuts that afternoon. She was deeply calm, dense at the core, as if her specific gravity was much increased in the couple of days since last I'd seen her. As solid as she seemed at the center, the edges where she met the world felt fuzzy. Her speech was slower and less precise than usual. The pitch of her voice was lower and the texture of it pebbly. Language did not seem to be the medium of choice between us that afternoon, so I let my fingertips speak instead, rubbing circles on her back and shoulders, stroking her hair, taking up her hand and holding it in mine. We were calm and blue and quiet, melting together into the world beyond those big translucent panes of glass.

After a while one of the nurses came around. "Your mom's had a little fever for the last couple of days," she told me. "I'm thinking the doctor should have a look at her."

My mother hadn't had a bladder infection since moving to Messenger House. I told the nurse that if she had another one, the doctor would authorize antibiotics over the phone. I was thinking, I must confess, of the Monday morning director's meeting at my new job, of my first day as a director.

"I don't think it's that," the nurse said. "I think she ought to be seen."

I felt the line that halved my psyche, daughter on one side, director on the other. Peace here and progress there. Stasis and frenzy. The journey inward and the world expanding out. I wanted to be big enough to contain the dialectic. I rubbed my mother's back and despaired of my ability to do so. I asked the nurse if there was a doctor who made house calls.

"Not until he's seen the patient in his office first," she said.

I explained to the nurse about my new job. I told her that I would leave work immediately after the meeting and catch the ferry home and take my mother to the doctor. That it wouldn't happen much before noon. I wanted to be centered, but inside I felt discouraged and distracted.

My mother lifted her chin. "What are you talking about?" she asked.

"About taking you to the doctor tomorrow, Mom."

"Oh," she said. "Am I sick?"

"You have a fever."

"Oh," she said.

The nurse left us. We sat. Around us, people moved and ate and argued, but we were all but oblivious of them. Once Virginia walked her wheelchair up to us and asked what we were doing, but our twosome would not easily extend to three that day, so she wheeled herself away. Finally, my mom picked up the old *National Geographic* magazine that had all this time been lying open on her lap. She turned the pages, pointing to particular pictures. Alligators in a swamp. Ice caves. Aborigines.

"Look at that," my mother said. "That's something, huh? So many things that could scare you, if you let 'em." She turned a few more pages. We looked at pictures. Then my mother closed the magazine. "I'm not afraid anymore," she said.

"That's good, Mom. I'm glad."

A little while later, I got up and told her I had to go home and make dinner. "If you're feeling better next weekend, you can come to Sunday dinner then," I said.

I could feel my mother gathering herself. I could feel the magnetism she exuded, trying to make me stay. "Will you come back tonight, then?" she asked me.

"Tomorrow," I told her. "I'll take you to the doctor tomorrow. We'll have lunch."

"Oh," my mother said. "All right."

I asked my mother if she wanted me to move her anywhere. She said no. I kissed her cheek and said goodbye.

"Are you coming back tonight?" she asked me.

"Tomorrow," I told her. "I love you, Mom."

My mother nodded. She smiled at me. By the time I reached the door to buzz myself out, she was leafing through her magazine again.

The call came a little after midnight.

My mother had gotten up and come out to the common room for a glass of water. The nurse walked her back to her room at the end of the hall and helped her crawl into her bed. My mother settled back into her pillows, took one deep breath, and then no more. It was the peacefulest, the most deliberate of deaths.

Fifteen minutes later, I knelt beside my mother's bed. Now everything about her face turned up, as if gravity itself had relaxed its pull. Her hand was still warm and supple. I had no doubt her spirit was still within whisper distance. I told her again and again how much I loved her. I told her that no matter what she encountered on her journey, the right direction was always toward the light. Every spiritual tradition says that, so it must be true.

I told her I was sorry for all the rocks that had made the road between us rough in life. I told her I believed we both had done our best. I wept from the bottom of my soul. I kissed her hand. Schuyler was there with us, a silent witness to our goodbye. At last I ran low on words and tears. I kissed my mother's forehead. She seemed to be smiling, a gentle little smile.

The way home lay past a sea cove. We parked the car and climbed down to the beach. The water was smooth and black, with just a faint hiss of tidal foam where it lapped the sand. The moon was big but not full and lay a silver path across the surface of the sea. To the great mother ocean, we prayed for my mother on her way.

54

goodbyes

Later that day, I called Maria and received instructions for the proper care of my mother's soul. For nine consecutive nights, we were to light a candle and say nine prayers. It was our chance to say everything to her we felt, everything we might have neglected to say before. At the end of the nine days of our Novena, we must release her to her journey. For three months, she would be with the angels, learning from them, and we must not distract her or call upon her in that time.

At the end of three months, we were to make a meal for her. Then, once again, to let her go, doing nothing in our ignorance or selfishness to bind her to this plane. After a year and nine days, my mother would become an ancestor. In celebration, we would prepare nine dishes and nine drinks and have a feast in her honor. We would say nine prayers and put her on our spirit tables. Thereafter, we might ask her help and counsel anytime.

We should be surprised by nothing that happened in those first nine days, Maria said.

What happened was, we grew close around our grief. We gave it shape and tenure. We took the opportunity to say everything that needed to be said, to feel all we needed to feel and release. Within the strict shape of the ritual, we were able to laugh sometimes, make light, and turn toward life. Nine days is long enough to be a passage and a process. We were not the same at the end as we were when we began.

This was our private ritual. Within the envelope of those nine days, I also made provision for a larger and more public farewell. By sheer grace, I was able to engage the small round chapel of the big downtown church to which we'd once belonged. I met with the associate minister, and explained to him about our beliefs. While I sought his skill as a pastor, I asked that he refrain from theological specificity. He graciously agreed. The service took place on Palm Sunday afternoon, on the seventh day of our Novena. In all, maybe thirty people turned up to say goodbye.

There was music. There were prayers. Then we gave people the chance to share memories of Anne. Schuyler spoke about the woman he had known only in the grip of dementia, in the last years of her life. He talked about the songs they'd sung together, the trips to Costco, the good times we'd had. My cousin Orky talked about the lively, beautiful young modern aunt who went to law school and smoked cigarettes and wore elegant clothes. My son, Ian, read Walt Whitman's "Out of the Cradle Endlessly Rocking," because it was one of his grandma's favorite poems. My mother's best college friend talked about their days in the sorority, and my mother's lawyer, a woman, talked about how Anne and her generation were groundbreakers in their field.

I knew from the start that I would have to speak, but at first it was not clear to me what it was I had to say or how exactly I was supposed to hold myself together. Then, over time, conviction grew in me. I would tell some of the hard home truths my mother and I had learned, not easily. The oldest of my mother's nieces and nephews were in their seventies. Their children, like me, were middle-aged. I would share our lessons, because their journeys might be easier for hearing them.

When my turn came, I gripped the lectern for support. My body grew sturdy as a tree, and I forgot it. My throat was full of tears and hesitations, but these, too, fell away. My voice, when I spoke, was loud and clear and forceful. I talked a little bit about the happiness we'd found in our last years together, about the blessings of living in the eternal present, as one must without memory. About my mother's courage and her pride and her terrible isolation. And then, because she wanted me to, I shared what we had learned together.

There are no prizes given for suffering alone.
If someone wants to help you, accept it.
If you need help, ask for it.
If you lack joy, seek it.
Do not try to hide from death or you will become invisible to life, as well.
Embrace both, so that you may live fully.

After her lessons were delivered, my mother left me. I managed to thank people for coming and invite them to join us for Chinese food at Chau's after the service. Then, standing between my husband and my son, I dissolved into my own sadness.

That night, at home, we continued with our prayers.

Several times in the course of the Novena, white clouds obscured my son's vision. On the last night of the nine, from nowhere, a tiny white moth appeared and flitted gaily all around me. I understood that it was my mother's last joke, though I'm not sure if it meant she always knew the truth about the butterflies, or was only now forced to acknowledge it. Whichever, the little creature was a delicious bit of levity. I took it as absolute proof that my mother's sharp wits had been restored to her. At length we said the last prayer and blew out the last candle. We embraced each other and said goodnight, Ian heading upstairs to his bed, Schuyler and I to ours.

Not too much later, Ian appeared at the door of our room. "Did one of you just knock on my door?" he said.

We told him we had not.

"It was Grandma then, saying goodbye," he said.

55

letting go of the branch/
an epilogue

In time of peace, the dusty plate-glass windows of main-street Bremerton, a shipyard boomtown on the Olympic Peninsula, are a wavery, reflective wall separating empty shops from empty streets. Up on the hill, the community college does its best to be a capital of culture. This gray June Saturday in the early 90's, it hosts a writers' conference. The featured guest is poet Denise Levertov. I am one of a cadre of lesser lights, there to teach workshops and judge contests. As usual, I am slightly resentful of how much easier the poetry judges have it, how many fewer words they must digest in order to come to their decisions. In the category of prose fiction, I've picked a clear if oddball winner and two runners-up of lesser quality from a pile of submissions so tall my eyes still hurt from having read it all. Neither the slow pace of the proceedings nor the stale refreshments would dishearten me quite so much if the sun had not been in hiding for so long.

Denise Levertov's reading is the conference's highlight and its very last event. To see Levertov in person is the reason I agreed to attend. My knowledge of her poetry is spotty, fruit plucked from anthologies, but I am still indebted to her for saving my sanity nearly twenty years before, when she wrote an essay in response to Anne Sexton's suicide that appeared in the more alternative of Boston's weekly tabloids. The rest of the culture, academic and popular alike, was intent on forging an imperative link between female creativity and self-destruction. Levertov cried foul, attacking the myth, defending the essential health of the impulse to create. Her essay lighted a dark time.

In person, her voice is prim, English-accented, with just the touch of a lisp, but there is a stringency to her language that cuts through the end-of-conference torpor. High intelligence, high standards, a comfortable eccentricity emanate from the slight woman at the lectern. I sit up straight and strain to hear, whimsical poems and smart ones, many with animals in them, poems that feed my skittish attention small treats of clarity. To end, she reads a few pieces that wrap the most ephemeral of perceptions in the simplest, most concrete words, poems that evoke the dance of faith and doubt with such rigor and such longing that I become aware, suddenly, of the movement of blood through my arteries, of the autonomic drumbeat of my heart. Suddenly, I am not weary anymore.

An hour later, Denise Levertov sits primly among sweat socks and empty Gatorade bottles in the backseat of my old brown Honda. She is wearing a finely woven straw hat and her hands are folded in a prayerful knot as I speed up the highway toward Bainbridge Island and a ferry sailing we might just make. Another respected poet, Madeline DeFrees, once Richard Hugo's protégée and always, probably unfairly, eclipsed by his fame, rides shotgun. I am giddily aware that I hold two formidable pilgrims, a lapsed nun and a convert to Catholicism, captive in my vehicle for the duration of the drive. The only possible gambit, I decide, is bold impertinence. I rehearse my line a few times silently, then say it out loud.

"Ladies, the price of this ride is a conversation about faith."

Whatever pretexts put them in my car in the first place disappear. This must be the discussion they secretly wished to have, because once begun, it rises up and rolls along with the force of a river following its proper course, a point-counterpoint examination of church as context and as discipline, necessary or not, the reciprocal baring of two quite different souls. It is an act of intimacy I am allowed to witness, yet one conducted gravely, with polite restraint. Once, hoping to give Denise in back more legroom, Madeline attempts to move her seat forward, but she grasps the wrong handle, releasing the seat back so that she swoons into Levertov's lap. Supine now, Madeline can no longer reach the lever that did the deed and we are moving much too fast for me to help her. Both women adjust to their altered positions with little pause in the talk and no lapse of dignity. Mother Church and Mother Nature inevitably come forward to plant the poles of a dialectic as important to the religious impulse as to poetry. Inside me, a bell rings as it would in Mass, to signal a holy moment. I hope I really was as speechless, as little intrusive as I remember being now.

My mother turned eighty in the fall of that year.

In short order, inevitably, the startup adventure died. By midsummer, 2000, I was without a mother or a job. Our little business, neglected through spring, was limp as a philodendron at the end of a long vacation. I missed my mother viscerally, the way one scans the skyline for an imploded building, or probes with one's tongue the pulpy hole where a tooth has just been pulled. Taking seriously the direction not to impede her journey, I did not call her back—*Mama, Mama, where are you?* —but kept silence and prayed for the progress of her soul.

Right after Christmas, when both of my children were home, I retrieved my father's ashes from the borrowed niche where he'd been squatting for a dozen years, combined them with my mother's in a dissolving urn, and at the morning turn of tide sent them off to sea together just as the rising winter sun painted the dark water gold.

When a year and nine long days had finally passed, I cooked a feast in my mother's honor that we all shared—Schuyler, my son, and I. After dinner we gathered at my boveda to put Anne's picture on it, drank champagne, and toasted her life on earth and her continuing adventure in other realms. We prayed. Warmth filled the alcove and our hearts, both a literal, measurable rise in temperature and the ambient sensation of almost overwhelming love.

After that, my mother began occasionally to appear in my dreams again, although she never spoke to me or looked me in the eye, just went about her business as if I were not there.

I was a challenge to Denise, I think. Most of her relationships in her last years were with younger poets whose work she fostered, with old friends or literary colleagues whose work she approved. After we met, she read the most recently published of my novels and did not admire it. Normally, that would have been sufficient reason to eliminate me from her circle of acquaintance, but Denise found some merit in me, or sensed some need that transcended literary style. Ultimately, she was as chastened by her rush to judgment as I was stung by it. We struck a peace that let us share some hours and something of ourselves, an afternoon tea that lasted long past dinnertime, a few lunches, excursions with mutual friends, little flurries of notes exchanged by mail. Her scrawl, I remember, had the elegant momentum of a bird just taking flight. We talked deeply and with great candor about writing and love and God. I learned about Denise that her natural inclinations and her convictions were often at odds. Apart from the sensuous appeal of the Church, I believe she became a devout and practicing Catholic because it was the hardest thing she could do. It was her way to choose the steeper road.

When I had to make a difficult decision concerning one of my children, Denise introduced me to Ignatius of Loyola's discernment exercises, through which one evaluates a course of action by ascertaining whether it induces feelings of consolation or desolation. It proved to be a wise and useful spiritual tool, and helped me make a choice I could both live with and defend. I was grateful to Denise for sharing it with me, though I could not help but wonder if perhaps she didn't find it a little too straightforward, a little simpleminded for her own use.

Rosi pirouettes about the kitchen, spinning from refrigerator to sink, sink to stove, on tiptoe, stretching to reach the highest cupboard shelves, crouching to retrieve a needed pan. She moves with the grace of a dancer, which she is, and the total absorption of one who is alone, which she is not, not really. I'm slouched in a straight-back chair against the wall, eating a not-quite-ripe nectarine and not quite thinking, either, simply hanging out after a trip to the hairdresser and the market on a hot afternoon in July. Rosi's hair is newly cut, straightened, and tinted into a gamine cap the color of a fruity Beaujolais. She may be a respected elder, religion-wise, but she is no frump. She hums a salsa tune and shimmies to it as she cooks. The ease that lets us ignore each other for the moment arises from being neighbors, or almost so. The madrinas have a new house, in East Oakland, and so do we.

Schuyler, Ian, and I moved to California just two weeks before the World Trade Towers fell in New York. The intervening year has been economically harrowing and spiritually rich. Our tradition is oral. At last we are on hand to learn by listening. After eleven months in Oakland, I am no longer the same person I was when I arrived, of this I'm sure, even though it would be hard to quantify the changes.

Two nights before, on my birthday, Rosi invited me to assist her at a misa for the first time. I kept notes for the client. At one point, with every one of my nerve endings at shivery attention, I sensed the presence of one of her ancestors and received a message on her behalf. This was a milestone. Within the Ile, it is one of Rosi's jobs to oversee the development of whatever spiritual aptitudes its members have. For the last eleven months, I have been one of the baby chicks assembled about her mother hen.

Now, in the kitchen, the scent of garlic sautéing rises from the pan. I, too, feel vaporous, a little strange.

Wooden spoon in hand, Rosi turns from the stove and looks at me, the way she might if I'd just said something provocative. As far as I know, I have not. She cocks her head. "You feel anything?"

For a moment, I interrogate my nerves, the surrounding air, then shrug.

"What was the last thing your mother asked you to do?" Rosi is focused now, her eyes fixed on me, her voice a third grade teacher's, strict: Where is your homework?

I interrogate the past.

"You don't remember, do you?"

"I do remember. On the last day, I went to see her in the afternoon. As I was leaving, she asked me if I was coming back that night. She asked me several times."

"Did you?"

"No."

"Why not?"

"I had to go home and make dinner. I had a new job. I told her I'd come back the next day."

"Why didn't you do what she wanted?"

"I did come back that night. I came back as soon as they called me. Her body was still warm."

"She knew," Rosi says.

"I sat with her for a long time. I held her hand and talked to her. Her spirit was still there, you know."

"It's not the same," Rosi says.

"No."

"You thought she was going to live forever." Rosi says this as if it is a new thought, just arrived.

I remember thinking my mother might live another five years, another ten. "Not forever," I say.

"You feel guilty," Rosi says.

For an instant, I hold the truth at bay. In my official version of events, there is no room for guilt. I did what I could. How could I know? Officially, I am guilt-free.

"You feel guilty," Rosi says again.

I accept the truth of it. The weight. Tears well up in my eyes. Actually, I feel twice-guilty, having disappointed my mother and my madrina both. "You're right. I do."

With a tilt of her head, Rosi points toward the kitchen table. Soft-voiced, she tells me, "Your mother is here."

I take a deep breath.

"Can you feel her?" Rosi says.

I shake my head.

Rosi nods. "Too light," she says, mostly to herself. To me, "Your mother wants you to stop feeling guilty. She wants you to forgive yourself."

Now that I've owned it, guilt covers me like a costume, like a shroud. It is dark and heavy and familiar.

"Did you hear me?" Rosi says.

"Yeah." I did hear, but guilt makes me feel like a crow hunched on a telephone wire, with wings too heavy to fly.

"This is important," Rosi says sternly.

"Yes." It is ten degrees hotter in the kitchen now. My eyes are burning.

"You need to say it," Rosi says. When I do nothing, she says so again.

Slowly and without much conviction, I do. "I forgive myself for not going back that night."

And something changes. The kitchen cools. Rosi nods. "That was it," she says. "Your mother's gone now."

I feel weak-kneed and nerveless, light. If I have forgiven myself, does this mean my mother has forgiven me?

. . .

"Faith's a tide," Denise wrote in one of her later poems. It is one of those lines that find their meaning when the reader is ready to understand. Faith has its rhythms, full and slack. For most of the past year, I have lived at high faith, weathering financial shipwreck, lighting signal fires on the beach to attract some dimly imagined rescue. I have sent a hundred copies of my résumé off in a hundred bottles and taken what little joblets came my way. My religious education has progressed if my career has not, and I have come to know and genuinely love the remarkable men and mostly women who make up our spiritual family. I have resisted the equation of faith with weakness. Not only have I believed that everything would eventually turn out okay, I have not wavered in my conviction that I was bound for the priesthood myself, that as soon as I could afford it, I would follow Schuyler's footsteps and make my ocha.

Now that the means are almost in the bank, doubt rushes in. When neither Schuyler nor I has steady employment, when there is so little security, how can I possibly proceed along this path? Every reason not to advocates itself, and does a fine job of it, too, being not just well spoken but comfortably familiar for one who is by heritage a third-generation agnostic, the daughter of a tribe proud of its resistance to belief. I have known for a long time I would be tested, I have expected this wavering, yet it is absolutely chilling when it comes.

Having been diligent, now I am derelict. I no longer sit at my boveda every day, or even every week. Walking past it, I glance quickly, then avert my eyes. Lately full of prayers, my mind empties of adoration. I try on the attitudes of a scoffer, tell myself jokes that discredit the premises of my chosen way. I resist the impulse to make chocolate chip cookies for Maria, who loves chocolate chip cookies. I have a dream about my mother. In it, she is perhaps sixty years old and we have to move back into the apartment where I was a child. The living room is swathed in funereal green curtains. I apologize for selling the furniture and tell my mother she will have to get a part-time job. The blue screen of death strikes my computer again and again. I lose data on a weekly basis. I cannot concentrate. It irritates me when Schuyler prays out loud.

At last I have a reading and the shells confirm it. I am at peril, afloat on a current of loss. My heart is breaking. I do not understand why.

When we moved to Oakland, it was important to find places to be alone outside. In due time, I came upon a little hill, always breezy, with a territorial view in all directions. Four huge old eucalyptus trees define the corners of a square on top of the hill, and a slender young one, barkless, stands inside. The largest of the four corner trees has a broad inward curve to the trunk that makes a perfect chair back. I was given to understand that this place was my refuge, that inside it I was free to pray or daydream, even to sleep, to surrender to my thoughts with no fear for my safety. I have lain on my back in the middle of the clearing and listened to crickets and birdsong, the rush of freeway traffic not too far away. I have heard the sudden silence that falls upon the twittering underbrush when the shadow of a hawk or a turkey buzzard passes over it. I have nestled against the rough bark of the old mother tree and been comforted. For a long time, the hilltop was built in to my morning run, but during my lapse of faith, I do not go there at all.

And then, at last, I do. The grass is longer and drier now than it was, and a dark red clover seems to have replaced the tiny orange wildflowers of early spring. Long strips of shed bark lie about the feet of the trees. The clearing does not reproach me for my absence. My backside still fits into the trunk of the old tree and I lean against her, feeling anxiety leach out of my body and into the earth until I am neutral and peaceful inside, a container with no contents, waiting to be filled. The next thing that moves is a blue jay, casting off from the branch of a nearby tree. For some time, he is in freefall, until he unfurls his wings to catch the little wind. I do not breathe until he does. A voice inside my head says, *If you leap from the branch but do not spread your wings, you will fall like a stone.* It is then I remember Denise, and her beautiful proof of the existence of God: "I have not plummeted." This is both how and when she made her way into this story. As I sat and remembered her, another, corollary phrase formed in my head. *If you don't let go of the branch, you will never learn to fly.*

I am a woman with many mothers, and I am just coming into my own.